PENGUIN BOOKS
WHOSE SAMOSA IS IT ANYWAY?

Sonal Ved is the group digital editor for *Harper's Bazaar India*, *Cosmopolitan India* and *Brides Today*. She was the first food editor at *Vogue India*. Her second cookbook *Tiffin* was listed in the *New York Times* as one of the must-have cookbooks for Fall 2018. Her words have appeared in food publications such as *The Guardian*, Saveur, Food52 and Thrillist. Apart from writing about food, she has also hosted several cooking shows for Tastemade.

PRAISE FOR THE BOOK

'The genius of India has always been its ability to take global traditions and influences and turn them into something uniquely Indian. Indian cuisine is the best example of India's ability to take the international and make it national. Sonal shows us, in this marvellous book, how India created one of the world's best cuisines through absorption and assimilation.'

—Vir Sanghvi, journalist and author

'True perspective for any cook to really have a strong relationship with food comes from understanding where the food comes from not just geographically but historically and culturally. This book is going to be a gift to many of those cooks seeking to elevate their relationship with food and make it more genuine.'

—Ranveer Brar, celebrity chef

'This book is the need of the hour; I have waited 20 years for someone to write it.'

—Kurush Dalal, archaeologist, historian, food anthropologist and raconteur

'A long overdue, refreshingly modern curiosity applied to the history of Indian cuisine. Sonal aptly brings her quirky and fun-spirited personality to the writing desk.'

—Garima Arora, chef; first Indian woman to win a Michelin star

'The Vogue India Food Editor begins by describing her highly-coveted lunchbox in school—with its paneer enchiladas and baby corn idlis—and how the 'tiffins' from Sindhi, Bohri and Marwari friends were an early learning experience. With this book she aims to explore "the undercurrents that lay in all those school meals that differentiated Indian cuisine" from others.'

—*The Hindu*

'Covering an expanse of history, from the Indus Valley Civilization to present-day India, a new book looks at global influences on our food.'

—*Mint Lounge*

'The scope of the book is breathtaking and research flawless. It will be especially valued by those who are humble enough to cast dogma about nationalism aside and be prepared to embark on a journey to understand what India is—and what it wants to be.'

—*Business Standard*

'*Whose Samosa is it Anyway?* is a guide for anyone who wants to go back in time and dive into the history of the dishes that dot their plate. It is an ode to a cuisine that, for years, remained on the fringes of the global culinary scene.'

—*The Better India*

WHOSE
SAMOSA
IS IT ANYWAY?

THE STORY OF WHERE 'INDIAN' FOOD REALLY CAME FROM

SONAL VED

PENGUIN BOOKS

An imprint of Penguin Random House

PENGUIN BOOKS

USA | Canada | UK | Ireland | Australia
New Zealand | India | South Africa | China

Penguin Books is part of the Penguin Random House group of companies
whose addresses can be found at global.penguinrandomhouse.com

Published by Penguin Random House India Pvt. Ltd
4th Floor, Capital Tower 1, MG Road,
Gurugram 122 002, Haryana, India

Penguin
Random House
India

First published in Viking by Penguin Random House India 2021
Published in paperback in Penguin Books 2022

10 9 8 7 6 5 4 3 2 1

The views and opinions expressed in this book are the author's own and the facts
are as reported by her, which have been verified to the extent possible, and the
publishers are not in any way liable for the same.

ISBN 9780143460060

Typeset in Adobe Garamond Pro by Manipal Technologies Limited, Manipal

www.penguin.co.in

*To my mother Asha, whose kitchen was my
first ground for research and whose support
(and lunches) have fuelled this project*

CONTENTS

INTRODUCTION

My curiosity to understand Indian cuisine began in the school canteen, my first exploration of food outside of home. The house I grew up in wasn't at all an ideal prototype to study the evolution of regional food. Like many urban Indian families, we were rooted in tradition—by way of Indian fasts and feasts—but an everyday meal at home was diverse, global and ahead of its time.

If there is one thing you should know about Gujarati families living in a metropolis in India, then it's the fact that they gave up traditional cooking and moved to Tarla Dalal-inspired meals over two decades ago. My school tiffin seldom came stacked with rotli, daal, bhaat and shaak, or as the cool kids called it, RDBS. It was a neat show of saucy paneer enchiladas, falafel stuffed inside bajra pitas, baby corn idlis, cream cheese pinwheel sandwiches, spinach and cheese havdo, things that made my tiffin the most covetable item in class— actually the second, after the back bench during a post-lunch chemistry class.

Unless I visited cousins in the heart of Kutch or Saurashtra, my exposure to Gujarati food remained the rice flour pankis that I ate at Swati Snacks, a restaurant in Bombay known for 'authentic' Gujarati cuisine (David Chang ate here). But even those meals were tinted with flavours inspired by Bombay. Occasionally, we ate hyper-traditional dishes, like a ghee-dotted bowl of dal dhokli followed by homemade shrikhand. Summers meant mango juice-based fajeto (sounds Mexican, but it's not), and aam panha. Winters meant gud papdi, lilva ni kachori and undhiyu, and the fasting season meant lots of faraal food—and that was more or less what I understood about my own region's cuisine.

In the nineties, when India was experiencing an internet boom, my table started to look different. The aloo parathas that we ate so often at dinner were nonchalantly served with an Ottolenghi dip (vaal instead of white broad beans) and amla chutney dotted on Martha Stewart's soft-shell tacos. Nigel Slater's ice-cream base was used to make our annual aam ras tub. So, to put it simply, the Ved kitchen was ever-evolving and was inspired by American–European influences before I was able to differentiate between what belonged to my ancestors and what we had been lugging along like Hailey Beiber and her Bottega.

Food at home left me with little matter to string together and understand what *Indian* food was all about before the various outside influences started accumulating over the course of time.

My palate had always sought wanderlust. In school, I marvelled at my Sindhi friend's tiffin that came brimming with macrolyun patata, or macaroni cooked in tomato gravy, which she ate with rotis; or at a Bohri friend's malida, a wheat-based sweet dish of Afghani origin. And I wondered how this Marwari friend's mom effortlessly made authentic khow suey that wasn't inspired from any cookbook but was an heirloom family recipe. My best friend, a Jain, though vegetarian on paper, skipped many vegetables. She taught me how to eat versions of potato-based dishes like pav bhaji, masala dosa and poha that did not have the root vegetable. And although I thank that experience for helping me understand the various shades of vegetarianism, I will never forgive her for making me try potato-less French fries. Yes, these were made of raw bananas.

Now that I think about it, there were many undercurrents that lay in all those school meals, those that differentiated Indian cuisine from other cuisines but also made it challenging for anyone to describe it in a line or two. I couldn't do it then, so I am trying to do it now, and that is why this book of 55,000 words.

As I began my research to understand the history of Indian cuisine, I had more questions than there were answers for. Did the European traders come before the Arab conquerors? Can you say cinnamon is an Indian spice even though it first grew in Sri Lanka on the Indian subcontinent? What are the origins of the quintessential chutney and samosa, or of the fruit punch, and how are they connected to India? Who taught us how to make ladi pav, and how did the Burmese khow suey land up on the wedding menus of Marwaris?

Experts who could answer my questions were spread across the world, and there were few books dedicated solely to this subject. As I set about to deep-dive into India's culinary history, I realized that the process was not going to be linear. Ingredients and dishes didn't show up in the Indian kitchen in a specific order or for a reason. They just did. Indian cuisine was layered, lacked chronology, and was tinted with myriad influences that I am just beginning to unravel.

The more I found out about the Indian kitchen, the more I realized that there is no such thing as a definitive Indian cuisine. Research papers, experts, historians and the internet had a lot of data, but my attempt was to streamline these ideas and—if I got lucky—to make it readable for my readers.

While writing *Tiffin*, my second cookbook, which compiles 500 recipes from the twenty-nine states and nine union territories of India, I had concluded that it was safe to say that there are as many hyper-local Indian cuisines as there are Indian states. And even states that share borders, like Punjab and Haryana or Karnataka and Goa, have similarities and dissimilarities, some of which can only be observed if you look at their kitchens through a magnifying glass. For each region in India has its own culinary narrative that speaks through its distinct dishes and kitchen staples. Sure, there were overlaps, but each cuisine packs within itself, textures, layers, ideas and historical nuggets so that all of Indian food cannot be pigeonholed together to say that there is one Indian cuisine.

As a starting point, I began to understand Indian cuisine by first determining the jarring points that separate our cuisine from another. Defining these factors that set it apart from another was a sweet spot around which I could gather my thoughts.

What I found out first was that there were many commonalities within the subcontinent, and these stood out more prominently as I moved away from the Indian subcontinent towards the West, making me realize how unexampled Indian subcontinental food truly is.

Even with the vast culinary diversities within regions, there were things that sewed them all together. Try and look at it as an intricate Sabyasachi lehenga. The lehenga may have mixed motifs, embroidery that doesn't rely on any one kind of thread, prints that vary in size, and colours that go from deep dark to poppy bright from one end of the dress to another—but when you look at it as a whole, it is downright delicious.

The first striking feature is that *Indian cuisine is based on an ancient civilization.* The Indus Valley and other civilizations—like those on the river Nile (ancient Egypt), the rivers Tigris and Euphrates (Mesopotamia), and the Yellow river (China)—are the oldest human clusters in the world. I've covered more about how the Indus Valley came into being in Chapter 1. This is to say that the first definitive chapter of Indian cuisine didn't originate out of an industrial revolution or from religious influences, wars, cultural exchanges or migration patterns, as with many other cuisines, but out of the sheer need for man to eat and survive. And therefore, it would be silly to compare it with modern haute French cuisine, which came about only in the seventeenth century, or with the latter-day Nordic, American or Australian cuisines, a mistake some young Indian chefs commit while trying to identify a way forward for Indian cuisine, which is at least 4,000 years old.

As, comparatively, newer cuisines have definitive timelines, their methods of cooking are sophisticated and their techniques well documented. But early Indian cuisine, or even the food cooked in non-urban Indian homes today, is rudimentary. It uses methods that are ancient—with recipes that are often not documented—which were developed over eras and not just a few centuries.

Another landmark feature of Indian cuisine is the *use of spices*. A discussion on Indian cuisine usually starts with spices, but doesn't end there. Spices are to Indian cuisine what the hashtag #wanderlust is to travel bloggers, a cliché but essential. It is impossible to cook an Indian meal without a fistful of masalas, most of which we have been using for centuries now. The generous throwing-in of spices into a sizzling tempering is one distinctive commonality across the country's cuisine, besides, of course, our habit of over-feeding guests with 'ek aur lijiye'.

The range of these spices too is vast. There are one-spice dishes, like basic subjis, which are based on a tempering of crackling mustard or cumin seeds, and there are refined kebabs and qaliyas that take up the flavour of up to sixty spices at a time. Spices are present in most savoury dishes cooked in the country, and some—like cardamom, nutmeg, cinnamon—can be found in desserts too.

In Chapter 4, I deep-dive further into the origin of our spices, which were crucial for building the flavour profile of our ancient dishes; and further, into how spice routes opened the Eastern world to the Western world, and vice versa. Indian spices, then, were what clickbait articles like 'Find your Disney Princess Name' are to a teenager on the internet. They led the West to us and exposed to them the beauty of sweet spices and their medicinal benefits, which for centuries were hidden in our kitchens. In the bargain, these spice-seekers created trade routes and caused a massive cultural explosion, eventually even invading the subcontinent and colonizing it.

Then come the *indigenous ingredients and equipment*; those that are native to this part of the world. In Chapter 1, I've spoken about ingredients that were found as molecular remains in various Indus sites, those like aubergine, ginger, gourd, and other produce that probably grew and were domesticated first in India. From the origins of agriculture in India, the meats that early Indians ate, and the cropping patterns and farming equipment—it is surprising that so much has evolved through the centuries, yet really not so much.

Through this book you'll trace the history of several local Indian ingredients as well as those that were borrowed from different parts of the world. Some flavours, like paan, saffron, amchur, imli, jaggery, asafoetida, kashundi, kalonji, kokum, ghee, turmeric and kewra, were the most striking to me.

Though not all of them originated in India, they exemplify distinct Indian flavour notes.

Our culinary equipment makes us stand apart too. Again, not all of these tools originated in the Indus Valley, yet even today they are core to traditional Indian cooking, and over the years have added to the complexity of our dishes. Take the Bengali shil nora, the north Indian sil batta, the Maharashtrian pata-varvanta, the Tamilian ammi and the Odia sila puaa, for instance. These Indian versions of the mortar-and-pestle find usage across the country. The speciality of these grinding stones is that you'll find them only in cuisines that started out in early civilizations and go as far back as the Stone Age. And this is exactly why there is also the molcajete and metate in Mesoamerican cultures.

The great Indian belan, splittingly similar to the Italian mattarello, but more slender, is commonplace across various kitchens in India. This didn't originate in India—in fact, it comes from the Etruscan civilization, around central Italy, somewhere between the eighth and third centuries BC. But universally, Indian cuisine is associated with the belan, and that it is distinctly accompanied by a circular rolling board or the chakla, which no other cuisine in the world uses.

Ask a rooted Indian chef, and they will tell you how important traditional equipment are for cooking certain dishes in a certain way. Though an urban home now has microwavable or stainless steel idli steamers, there are still a few homes in a village in Kerala making the pillowy soft Ramasseri idli in voluptuous clay pots lined with cloth. Their urli, an open-mouthed utensil, promises that the curry won't ever burn. The murukku press pushes down strings of dough to make the Gujarati or Maharashtrian chakli, or the Tamil murukku, and is almost as precious to our kitchen as the zoodle-maker is to a vegan blogger on YouTube.

Many Indian equipment were also woven into mythology and folk tales, and this makes us hold on to them even more closely. Like the curd churner, which is described in scriptures or depicted in paintings of Lord Krishna. Krishna was known to have a penchant for home-churned white butter and, in fact, was endearingly called 'makhan chor', or the butter thief.

Paintings of Krishna depict the great Indian matki, the epitome of classic Indian design. Not only is the matki the most important aspect of the Indian festival of Janmashtami, but also, a kitchen in India without this clay pot that stores and cools water at the same time is unimaginable. The design idea of preserving water in porous clay so it remains chilled in our tropical weather still remains relevant, centuries after it was first used as far back as 2300 BC in the Indus Valley.[1] We know this thanks to the remains found on the Indus sites. The same can be said about the lota, the scooped-neck tumbler that has stood the test of time. The matka and lota are both so clever. The lota's curved neck makes it easy to hold between the fingers; it is practical—each member in the family has his or her own lota—and symbolic. In Vedic society, the lota became an important symbol of Brahmanical puritanism.

Then comes the masala dabba, a sophisticated box that contains smaller containers of spices. It may have entered our kitchens only a few hundred years ago, and no one knows who designed it or where it came from. My guess is that it may have started as a wooden or clay box, later moving towards stainless steel. The circular dabba is filled with katoris of basic spices like cumin powder, coriander powder, mustard, turmeric, asafoetida and fenugreek. And, depending on which part of the country you are from, it will also hold garam masala, whole spices, panch phoran and other combinations.

Our habit of eating with our hands is another signature trait we share with cultures in certain parts of Asia, Africa and the Middle East, and in India it had the sanction of Ayurveda, which has described its multiple benefits. It starts with the fingers being able to identify the food's temperature and the nerve endings in the fingers alerting the brain to begin the digestion process. Besides, each finger represents one of the elements of the body: fire, earth, water, air and ether, and their coming together ensures the body's elements stay balanced.[2] Further, the manner of using the hand and the fingers for eating is based on mudras (hand positions derived from yoga). Apart from this, meals were usually served on banana leaves, which was a sustainable practice as the leaves were then inexhaustible and mainly contained polyphenols, a characteristic cancer-preventing agent found in plant-based foods.

Today, many of these signature Indian culinary traditions still exist in a more refined manner across the continent. Although eating on leaves or with fingers may have given way to crockery and cutlery, and the rustic kitchen tools have been replaced by contemporary food processors. One thing that has constantly happened through the centuries is the evolution of Indian cuisine, and that is what I aspire to trace through this book.

While the heart of *Whose Samosa Is It Anyway?* is about Indian food, the book extends towards the subcontinent too, since the map of India was drastically different then from how we see it today. The features described above don't just belong to India as we now know it now. And so, a fair way to describe Indian cuisine is less as 'cuisine of India' and more as 'cuisine of the Indian subcontinent'.

The book looks at Indian food by examining the Indian civilization in all its grandeur. The Indian subcontinent was a large body of land spread across a part of Persia in the west to almost all of China in the east. It had a motley of external influences streaming in with the traders and the invaders that set foot on the land, with the wars and truces, the royal kitchens, the religious doctrines. And all this shared history paved the way to make the cuisine what it is today.

I speak more about this in the chapters to come, starting from the breaking down of the earth's landmass into continents, the coming together of the Indus Valley civilization, and moving on to the various tribal and organized kingdoms that ruled the land at different points in history. Sometimes these 'Indian' dynasties may have spread all the way across Central Asia. As highlighted in the book, it is important to accept that each era of human history—be it the Indus Valley civilization period, the Vedic age, or the Brahmanical society all the way up to the

Mughal era—spread across centuries and what the people ate differed not only across but also within eras.

An experiment I highly recommend before we begin the book is to imagine Indian cuisine as a kadai. Into it we will add a variety of spices, meats, vegetables and produce found on various terrains—sea shores, mountains, rivers, meadows, plains, hills, deserts and the cities that make India—and now know that this cauldron will be stirred repeatedly, as new visitors and migrants trickle in and create new dishes and ideas.

As a starting point to understand the history of Indian cuisine, I begin around 4,000 years ago, when the Indus Valley civilization formed on this side of the world. Food from the early stages of the Indus Valley settlements was quite different from what we understand as Indian cuisine today. But interestingly, it was not too different too.

Now, the Harappans ate just like a cross-fitting millennial: a healthy dose of Indian superfoods like barley, amla, millets, honey, curd, various plants and meats. These were eaten in a rustic, intense form, such as coarsely ground or turned into a mushy gruel, or even raw. We know this from the research carried out by archaeologists on Indus sites like Harappa and Mohenjo-Daro, where fossils of grains, pulses, vegetables and animal bones have been identified, giving us a peek into what the food of early Indians was like. The most astonishing of these discoveries is their well-defined agriculture and food distribution system. There is a lot more about this in Chapter 1.

Our meals today are an interesting mix of 'what grows indigenously in India' such as a sorghum salad and 'borrowed influences' like a topping of a HASS avocado or an Italian burrata that the same salad now has. Similarly, throughout history, the food of our ancestors involved exchanged culinary ideas with other cultures and sharing of ingredients, recipes and agricultural know-how, which all ultimately was churned into one wholesome cuisine.

Though popular history tells us that structured (via barter or money) exchange began much later when the trade routes opened, Indus Valley researchers believe that not all remains found on the Indian subcontinent were native to this part of the land. Take something as basic as rice or pork, for an example. These were first domesticated in Southeast Asia, before early Indians began eating them. Conversely, oilseeds like linseed and sesame were primitive Indian subcontinental crops, which spread outside the region way before official trade routes opened up.

We do not have confirmed knowledge of who the successors to the Indus Valley civilization were, but for the sake of moving forward, let's just say they were the Aryans. The word 'Aryan' comes from the Aryas tribe, nomads who lived around the steppe grasslands of the Ural mountains in Russia.[3] Due to climatic changes in the region, they moved to as far as Ireland in the west and India in the east, exerting their supremacy on the basis of their light skin colour. While over 4,000 years have passed since this phenomenon may have occurred, researchers have still not been able to attest if there ever was a clan that descended to northern India, committed mass warfare and reduced the Indus Valley settlements to dust, or if it is just a legend.

Our knowledge of food from this period, therefore, remains sketchy, as not much about the Aryan diet is traceable. But we do know one thing—that like the earliest Indians, the Aryans too were a pastoral people. After the Indus Valley civilization and the so-called Aryan invasion, the pot of Indian cuisine was stirred as a result of the various religious influences that emerged in India. I cover this in depth in Chapter 2.

In brief, three early religions—Hinduism, Buddhism and Jainism—collectively made changes in the prehistoric Indian diet over the course of the centuries that came after. The text of their scriptures laid out detailed dietary rules for the followers of their religions. The four Vedas influence and explain a lot about why we eat, what we eat and the way we eat, even today.

The transformation of the Indus society into a Vedic society was an organic one. Knowledge of this introduced me to a whole new idea of how an early Indian may have lived. If the Indus society was rudimentary, the advent of the Vedas shows a more refined scenario. Sure, there are mentions of the same foods found in the Indus Valley civilization, but the later Vedic period spotlights many more ingredients and items that could be treated as predecessors of several Indian dishes found today. One example is the apupa, which roughly translates to 'grain pancake', which perhaps became the malpuas of early India. Besides, there is mention of whole-grain cakes, milk-based mithais, fruit juices, oilseeds and several dairy products that are not drastically different from what we stock in our kitchens today.

The Vedas, which were handed down through centuries, as well as the Ramayana, Mahabharata and other Indian scriptures mention food ingredients that help me understand why Indians eat certain foods keeping in mind the seasons, religious doctrines and so on. Hindu scriptures are a good starting point to gauge which indigenous foods might have been part of the early Indian diet. Some of these scriptures mention sesame, linseed, mango, cucumber, the Indian jujube, bael, gourds, lotus stalk, lemon, and mustard seeds, confirming their Indian origins. There are many more, and I have explored them in Chapter 2.

The early days of the Indus Valley civilization coincide with the Vedic period, and we know this thanks to the food-ingredient fossils found from this era. The basic ingredients and dietary rules are similar in some of the phases of these civilizations, but as the Indus civilization matured, moving from rudimentary crops to curries, gruel and breads, so did the food descriptions in the Vedas. From mere mention of crops in the earlier texts, the later texts move to deeper descriptions of the eating habits of early Indians, the dos and don'ts, cooking techniques, and the importance of cattle and agriculture. We unearth more details and affirm that both the Indus and Vedic societies were predominantly pastoral and agrarian, and for a while may have gone hand in hand.

Early Indian cuisine not only developed around the availability of ingredients, it also fleshed out the rules of cooking which apply even today, like mixing certain ingredients and avoiding certain pairings—for example, milk and onion were never eaten together. Utilizing an animal from nose to tail and eating seasonal were the other rules.

With Hinduism and its caste system, came new culinary traditions. Each of the four castes had a sui generis cuisine of its own, and practices of food-sharing and cooking rituals highly depended on these rules. These rules shaped cuisines in India from north to south. For instance, the Brahmins, who were the highest caste, did not accept food from the lower castes, and the same can be said of the Kshatriyas and Vaishyas, who accepted food and water from the higher castes but not from those born lower in the caste hierarchy.

This system played out in the matter of access to resources too. For example, Brahmins ate 'pakka' or pure food items, like milk and ghee, while the lower castes did not have access to these. Onion and garlic were forbidden for the higher castes (much as they were for the Jains), and they had a distinct cuisine, depending on where they lived. For instance, even now the Maharashtrian Brahmin's food habits are different from that of the south Indian Tamil Brahmin. The Saraswat Brahmin of western India ate differently from the Saraswat Brahmin of Kashmir. The Brahmins ate or forbade meat depending on which region they lived in. The Kshatriya or the warrior clan mostly ate meat, and Vaishyas (traders) mostly did not, with exceptions among both.

The lowest in the ladder, the Dalits, shaped their food preferences on the basis of two factors—survival and leftovers.

They did not have direct access to certain foods, dairy or water, whether from the plains, deserts or mountains, and therefore their cuisine developed out of their resourcefulness. The upper castes did not eat pork or beef, so these inevitably became a part of Dalit cuisine. It is ironical that Dalits are now being victimized by upper-caste vigilantes who want to stop cow slaughter; the food that the Dalits eat are a result of not being left with any choice by the same upper castes centuries ago.

Basic Dalit meals comprised grains, flour rotis and offal, and seldom fresh produce. They utilized the blood, head, trotters and organs of animals, the idea being not to waste anything.[4] Each sub-community within this lower caste had its own practices. For example, with time the Mahars were distinguished as Mrutaharis (those who eat dead animals), the Musahari in UP and Bihar were noted for their taste for rat meat, and the Valmikis were dependent on joothan, or leftovers from the upper castes.[5]

Food for the upper castes was mainly shaped by what the Hindu scriptures said. In the Upanishads, food was referred to as 'prana', or the source of energy, and nothing explains the 'you are what you eat' adage better than the food–mind–body connection mentioned in these. Though in the Mahabharata and Ramayana, one doesn't find food references the way they are dropped in folk tales, poems and scriptures of this period. Vidura in the Mahabharata serves Krishna a green leafy vegetable, which ever since is known as 'Vidura-saag'. In the Ramayana, we have Ram's encounter with Shabari, who feeds him ber or jungle berries. Sita and Draupadi were both known to be great cooks, and in one retelling of the Ramayana, there is a story of how a piece of bread made by Sita reached Lanka via a crow. Ravan ate the bread and was struck by her culinary prowess.

We also know how Lord Krishna loved dairy, from the imagery we see even today in paintings. Besides, the Puranas mention his other favourite foods like misri (chunks of sugar). In one of the Krishna stories, his childhood friend Sudama is seen bringing him a handful of rice as an offering. These are perfect depictions of what people may have eaten in this period.

This is also when the concept of annakut comes into being, and you'll find mentions of this in the Puranas again. This annual feast traces back to a time when Krishna asked his disciples to worship the Govardhan mountain, situated in the Mathura district of Uttar Pradesh. They did so by building a mountain of food, which was believed to never run out.[6] Another story goes that annakut came into being because Krishna lifted a hill to shelter people from Indra's wrath. The word 'annakut' itself comes from two words, 'anna' (food) and 'kut' (shortage). This spread is characterized by a pool of grains, vegetables, pulses, mounds of savoury and sweet rice, buttermilk, puris and several fried savouries and sweets. It is also a beautiful example of the temple food of India, which is a unique cuisine in itself, with no parallels elsewhere in the world, except some South Asian countries. I explore more of these connections and references in Chapter 2 to show how the advent of Hindu rituals affected Indian food.

Besides the Vedas, Buddha's teachings and the Jain Agamas provided strict culinary guidelines on what one could eat and laid down dietary taboos. Jainism was really India's first vegetarian movement, with dietary rules that haven't been diluted even after 2,600 years. Based on the basic parameter of eating in a manner that causes no harm to other living organisms, it branches out into finer detail, developing a whole new side of Indian cuisine. Jain vegetarianism was different from Hindu vegetarianism. The former was connected to the cosmic repercussions of consuming meat, whereas the latter was more concerned about the godliness in animals and other forms and rules of purity.

The influence of Hinduism and Jainism on Indian cuisine leads me to the third early religion that impacted Indian food deeply. Prince Siddhartha Gautama's Buddhism spread across several parts of the subcontinent. He was born in Lumbini in Nepal, and his last days were spent in Bodh Gaya in Bihar, India. The Buddha introduced his followers to basic dietary rules, mostly tilting towards ascetic abstinence. Buddhist scriptures lead us from the early days of Prince Gautama, still in his royal abode, when he indulged in lavish meals comprising fresh fruits, wild meats, sweetmeats and grains, to a monk who would survive on a meal of whatever was put in his bowl.

Unlike Jains, certain Buddhists ate meat. Buddhist doctrines didn't entirely forbid one from eating non-vegetarian food. But this depended on the school of Buddhism one followed. The Theravada school of thought allows monks pork, chicken and fish, as long as the monk was certain that no animal was killed for his personal consumption but was simply offered an already-cooked meal. Mahayana Buddhism is a rather strict form where no kind of meat is allowed, whereas Vajrayana Buddhism allows meat and even consumption of alcohol.[7] These sects didn't have much of a direct impact on Indian cuisine. However, Asian cuisine (Japanese, Korean, Chinese) at large was impacted by the Buddhist way of eating. In fact, inside the Seisho-ji temple in Tokyo, a restaurant at the foot of Mount Atago called Daigo, shojin ryori cuisine can be found. It draws inspiration from Buddhist vegetarian ways and in 2009, the restaurant got two Michelin stars.

The Buddha instructed his followers to eat anything that was put in their bowls, including meat. Scriptures, paintings and tales from this period help us understand what ingredients were available during then. My biggest takeaway is the lotus that is seen repeatedly in Buddhist relics. In the *Anguttara Nikaya*, the Buddha compares himself to a lotus. Obviously, the flower played an important role in the Buddhist way of life, and perhaps may have been cooked from stem to seed since the sixth century. So much for foxnuts (makhana) and lotus root chips being revered as new-age superfoods.

On the other hand, Jains weren't allowed to eat anything that had life—'jiva'—in it, and that is how serious vegetarianism got introduced to India. This also forever changed the way we ate, where meat wasn't the central component of a meal.

Apart from religion, royal dynasties based in India have added a lot to Indian cuisine. Before the European travellers came to this part of the subcontinent, several invasions throughout Indian history brought in new kings and their harems. They brought their own way of life, which kept getting tipped into the kadai of Indian cuisine, like milk in roux while making béchamel sauce—bit by bit. Though smaller kingdoms existed in various parts of the subcontinent, well-defined Indian kingdoms, like the Nandas, Mauryas, Guptas, Pandyas, Cheras, Kushanas and Kadavas, came in quick succession through the centuries and had distinct culinary ways of their own.

Scriptures played an important role even here, in identifying the role of food in the kitchen. Take for instance the *Arthashastra*, which was originally written on palm leaves around the first millennium BC. It throws light on the food habits of the Mauryan kingdom, among the most ancient in India. While writing Chapter 3, I discovered the meats that they ate, the drinks they devoured, and the ingredients in their kitchens. Each reign brought with it a new dimension. Overall, the Mauryan way of life and habits were similar to those of the ancient kingdom of Persia.[8] From the literature of this period we can get an idea of early ingredients like ghee, soma, curd, milk and honey, which belonged to Indian cuisine, as we have discussed at the start of this chapter. The Mauryans were a meat-eating society and their menu featured everything from deer and antelope to porcupine and tortoise. Animal sacrifice was common. A lot of insight into the Mauryan way comes from the *Arthashastra*, written by Chanakya aka Kautilya, a statesman from the court of a Mauryan king.

Similarly, *Manasollasa,* authored by the western Chalukya king Someshvardeva III (AD 1126–AD 1138) reveals the food habits of the Chalukyas.[9] One nugget is that of thirty varieties of fish that were recreationally fished by the royals. We find, for example, mention of chickpea, cooked rice and roasted flour balls used as bait, the size of the rope used for fishing, methods of filleting the fish (heads must be cut away) and preservation techniques (salting).[10] There are also vague descriptions of preparations that correspond to the current idli, poli, shrikhand, laddoo, dosai and vadai in these scriptures. There is a lot more non-vegetarian than vegetarian fare mentioned, allowing us to imagine the ancient royal kitchen of the time.

The north Indian Ramayana remains an important scripture that opens up a world of feasts and folklore, set in an ancient Indian kingdom. Sita's kitchen, the symbolism of the ingredients mentioned in the ancient texts, and the food references in the Mahabharata let me understand Indian cuisine from a mythological perspective. Minor food references spill through in lesser-known texts like the *Naishadha Charita,* authored in the twelfth century; this is a Sanskrit poem on the life of king Nala of Nishadha, an Indo-Aryan tribe, and it mentions the cooking and consumption of a meal comprising meat, roots and fruits.

For the most part, religious doctrines and scriptures, and rules made by the king went hand in hand, since royalties adapted and prescribed to the way of life suggested by their religion. For example, Ashoka's reign was influenced by the ways of the life of the Buddha, since Ashoka himself became a Buddhist.

The Cholas with their rich Sangam literature introduced us to several ingredients and their varied uses. Texts and poems from these eras also give us a picture of the ancient Indian markets, the systems of exchange, and food storage and distribution, providing us with a slice of the everyday life of those times.

Ancient dynasties were spread across the country. So, we have the Vijayanagar and Tanjore royal kitchens in the south, the Maratha kitchens of the west, the Marwari and Mewadi kitchens of north-west India, the kitchens of the Delhi Sultanate and the Mughals in the north, and those of the royal families of Odisha and Tripura in the east. And together, they form a beautiful picture of royal Indian cuisine.

This is when extravagance and finesse were added to the rustic ways of the Indian kitchen. You'll read more about this in Chapter 5, where I talk about my discovery of a variety of unique recipes and ingredients that emerged out of royal homes. While it was the temple cuisine that got the rituals of purity and food sanctions in place, it was the food of the royals that brought in the strict rules of food safety and systematic distribution of culinary goods.

It was in the royal kitchens that dishes like many mithais, chaats, kebabs and curries were fine-tuned, where meats began to be slow-cooked and smoked delicately, where niche ingredients like screwpine water and edible silver and gold came to be used, and where desserts became a common feature of the Indian meal. Take, for example, veshta, a besan-based dish that goes all the way back to the Chalukya dynasty, or the laddige from Vijayanagar,[11] to the refined sweets like seviyan ka muzaafar that emerged from the Mughal kitchen—royalty added nuance that Indian cuisine may have previously lacked.[12]

The next shift came with the traders and invaders who started pouring into our shores. I want to talk about this with a personal story. I understood the impact of trade on a cuisine in school from a friend who used to bring in a dish of elbow pasta swimming in a tomato 'subji' in her tiffin. It was to be eaten with rotis. Now, I assumed it was one of those Indo-western combinations brown moms are notorious for cooking on days when fresh vegetables may not be available. But it turns out this was a part of her 'authentic' Sindhi repertoire, passed down from one generation to another. On researching its roots, it turns out the recipe may have come about after Sindhi merchants, who were among the first traders during the British time, began to interact and trade with the West. On their trips home they may have brought back packets of macaroni. The women of the house didn't know what to do with it, so they ended up making an Indian-style curry with it, leading to a dish called macronyul patata, or macaroni with potatoes.

Macronyul patata is just one example of how the advent of foreign ingredients in any kitchen is one of the major ways for any cuisine to evolve. And while early immigrations, invasions and religious doctrines led to changes in Indian cuisine, it wasn't until trading became common that Indians started to cook using these ingredients often.

As a concept, exchange of food ingredients (what you can also call trade), predates medieval and modern civilization. We know this from the early Indus Valley days when there was barter of toys, seals, jewellery, pottery and other items, all the way across the continent with the Mesopotamian civilization. So, it is safe to say that trade and commerce have been an important aspect of human evolution throughout Indian history. The Ramayana, for instance, contains words like vikraya (sale), mulya (price) and panya (merchandise). Then we have the existence of an entire caste that trades—the Vaishyas. We see exchange as a recurring theme in ancient Indian history.

But with respect to large-scale trade of food and food ingredients, the most profound change happened in the fifth century BC, when European travellers came eastwards in search of spices, silks and stories. In Chapter 4, we discover how these travellers went back home with stories about the 'charming' Indian subcontinent. And their poetry and writings described a plethora of food ingredients like fruits, spices and grains. Alexander's mammoth invasions in the east brought with him his ways, his people, and knowledge of his culture, produce and cuisine. The Macedonians took back a slice of the Indian subcontinent for Europe, Hellenistic colonies spread across the world and kept the exchange of ideas flowing, thereby shaping the way our kitchens look.

The Silk and Spice Routes, and much later the great Grand Trunk Road, opened the floodgates of ingredient exchange between the Indian subcontinent and many other regions of the world in a more profound way. Though India had always been a hub of culture, ever since the ancient cities of Pushkalavati, Taxila, Madurai and Patliputra (Patna) buzzed as popular international markets, these routes brought more structure to civilizations, trade and exchange.

Besides, the geographical positioning of India made it an ideal centre of global trade. The Indo-Gangetic plain in the north of the subcontinent was connected to the ports on the Bay of Bengal. By the end of the Mauryan empire (322 BC to 185 BC), the Ganges was used as a channel for trade, and routes were also established by early migrations of Hindus, Buddhists and Jains from the Ganges regions across South Asia.[13] These routes became the finer links feeding into the Silk Route for travellers moving from Xi'an to Kabul or Mashad, from Bukhara to Samarkand to Rome, as well as the other way around to the Indus.[14] They also became core to the exchange of ingredients in and out of the Indian subcontinent, resulting in rice becoming an important grain in the Islamic word, the apricot finding itself in Georgia in the Caucasus, and apples reaching as far as America (although much later), or cardamom finding its way to Guatemala. Crops migrated from their places of origin and spread across the world through trading routes.

Much later, Christopher Columbus's Columbian Exchange comes into picture. His European voyages that began in 1492 stoked the development of Indian cuisine in the most profound way. As a result of this European exploration of the earth in the fifteenth and sixteenth centuries, the world saw a massive globalization of food ingredients. Hundreds of new plants and animals were introduced to different parts of the world, and this changed the face of Indian kitchens too. One such ingredient is corn, the West's gift to other continents, along with potato, cassava, sweet potato, tomato, pumpkin, squashes, pineapple and chilli peppers. And the West got a taste of watermelon, yam, sorghum, millets, coffee, okra, banana, orange, lemons, and other citrus fruits via the East.[15]

Chapter 4 further explores travellers like the Portuguese, the French and the Dutch, who came to Indian shores as visitors, traders or missionaries and later colonized the land and became conquerors. Their long stays brought in a different culinary know-how, which they tipped into the already bubbling pot of Indian culinary soup. These changes made our pantries expand, introducing new techniques and farming practices, and new dishes and adaptations slowly began to weave a thicker fabric of Indian cuisine.

Take, for instance, the introduction of a range of fruits, dried fruit and nuts from Central Asia, cooking techniques like the making of kebabs, or the slow-cooking of ingredients or the use of the tandoor, the art of making flatbreads or preserving sweet fruits as murabbas—these are just a handful of things that weren't indigenous to India but borrowed. Central Asia gave us numerous seemingly Indian dishes, from falooda, which literally translates to 'shredded' (referring to the noodles in it) and which travelled to India from Shiraz in Persia and has stayed here for over 1,000 years, to my most favourite story, that of the great Indian samosa. This is also the reason why the book is called what it is. Samosas are named after samsa, the Central Asian pyramidal savoury pastry, because of their shape, and the word etymologically derives from the Persian word 'sanbosag'.[16] You'll catch a lot more of this story in Chapter 3.

I think Central Asian culinary influences had the greatest impact on Indian food, especially on the regional cuisine of the Kashmir region. This cuisine is primarily divided into the Pandit style of cooking (which uses asafoetida and curd), and the Muslim style of cooking (which uses onion and garlic). Meat is relished by both communities. A traditional Kashmiri cook is known as a waza even today, and may or may not have his lineage tracing back to the original chefs who migrated from the area around Samarkand and other parts of Central Asia in the early fifteenth century as a part of Timur's entourage. These wazas shaped the future of Kashmiri cuisine by designing a meal known as wazwan, which historically featured dishes such as rista, rogan josh, dhaniwal korma, aab gosht and a number of others, which still live on.[17]

Further, Central Asia (mainly Persia) shaped Parsi cuisine too. Parsis, who form less than one per cent of India's population, have a distinct cuisine of their own, which adds to the diversity of the Indian plate. They were initially direct descendants of the Zoroastrians from Persia, a group who fled their country around the eighth century and moved to India.

They settled in Gujarat, but their eating style remained on the fringes of their Persian diet. Thanks to them, a variety of egg-based dishes were introduced to Indian cuisine, like akuri or spicy scrambled egg; picnic poro, a variety of omelette; and kuku, which is their version of the frittata. Some of these are trademarks of the Persian way of combining eggs with vegetables.

Adding to this list are the Mughals, who settled in India and ruled for over 300 years and influenced Indian cuisine greatly. It is a known fact that the Mughals ate lavishly and introduced a riot of colours, textures and fragrances to the Indian kitchen that were not present before their advent. Their cuisine itself was a borrowed platter of influences that ranged from the Turkish to the Afghani and Persian, which effortlessly amalgamated with the Kashmiri, Punjabi and Deccan cuisines of India. They traded with the Portuguese, which means they had access to a wide range of fruits, vegetables and ingredients, which until then had no presence in the Indian kitchen. They taught the Indians how to refine their rice-based dishes and curries, chronicled culinary feats in manuscripts like the *Alwan-e-Nemat* and the *Nuskha-E-Shahjahani*. They elaborated on methods of cleaning fish, softening meat and colouring food using fresh vegetable and floral juices. You'll read more about this and its derivative, the even finer Awadhi cuisine, in Chapter 3. It gets its name from Ayodhya—the birthplace of the god Ram—which was then a Mughal province and therefore extracted ample culinary inspiration from the Mughal kitchens.

What some Europeans (like the French and Dutch colonists who settled in India for decades) did for Indian cuisine is not chronicled enough, but there are some influences from them that could be gleaned, which you can read about in Chapter 4. We do know one thing with certainty though, that they took back spices and condiments such as pepper, mustard and cumin, and added hints of these to their own native cuisines. The Portuguese and the British, on the other hand, influenced Indian cuisine in a way that independent cuisines like Goan-Portuguese and Anglo-Indian developed within the bigger umbrellas of Indian cuisine, as a result of the long stay of these visitors. You'll read more about this in Chapter 4.

The Portuguese influence on Indian cities like Goa, Kolkata and Kochi was massive, considering that those were key ports, and worked its way into the Indian kitchen. The New World exploration by the Portuguese led to an exchange of goods and produce, which multiplied in the centuries to come. They were avid traders, who not only traded in the local bounty but also sold the ingredients they gathered from their travels to Central and South America in the east and the Indian subcontinent. Their contributions to the Indian kitchen included the Mayan civilization's red beans and maize, the Inca empire's sweet potato, tomato, groundnut, chilli and tapioca. The most interesting debate that comes out of this is the emergence of guava in the Indian kitchen. In some parts of India it is called 'peru' even today, after the country of its origin in South America. Though the English translation of *Ain-i-Akbari* speaks about 'amrud' centuries before this (experts believe this could be the translation of 'pear', which was also called by the same name).[18] You'll read a lot more about the history of Indian fruits in Chapter 4.

Lastly, the British colonists impacted Indian cuisine, but not as deeply as the Persians, the Mughals or the Portuguese. They spent over 200 years on the subcontinent and stirred the Indian kadai in several ways. Chapter 4 and the Conclusion speak of the influence of the British on Indian cuisine, the emergence of the hybrid Anglo-Indian cuisine, how the British learnt the use of spices from us, took back chicken tikka masala, introduced whisky, tea, coconut cookies, finger sandwiches and sponge cake to India, how they made us ditch floor-style seating and moved us to dining tables, introduced us to porcelain and China plates, and more.

And so, India's colourful cuisine developed over 4,000 years in a tremendously layered manner ever since its inception in the Indus Valley civilization. It was non-linear in terms of chronology, colourful with many influences, aromatic with many ingredients and mysterious.

I invite you to take this journey with me, which starts with a prehistoric India moving through various influences that shaped it, to become the home of the fine cuisine that we see today in swish restaurants from Mumbai to Manhattan. It's the result of thousands of years of migrational history, conquests, exchanges and stories of displacement that played catalyst to create this not-so-definitive cuisine we call 'Indian'.

1

THE INDUS VALLEY

It's a hot afternoon in Mumbai and I'm at the book-filled apartment of Professor Shereen Ratnagar. She's a veteran archaeologist in the city, who has written several books on Indus life. We're cooling off by eating cold local grapes from a bulky terracotta bowl that she's placed in front of me, as we chat about what the food of the people of the Indus Valley civilization was like. Until this point, I didn't know that grapes, like the ones I was eating, were probably a snack even for the Harappans around 4,000 years ago, when they unwound in their mud-brick homes during summers, in between harvesting cereals and pulses. A vision of early Indians snacking on grapes that may have looked nothing like the domesticated fruit we eat today pops up in my mind. I imagine them eating fruit off a similar open-mouthed terracotta bowl.[1] Probably discussing if the gazelle meat from last evening's hunt will be enough for dinner tonight.

According to the National Horticulture Board, grapes were first introduced in India around AD 1300 by invaders from Iran and Afghanistan.[2] But Ratnagar is convinced that they existed in India even earlier, perhaps in the latter half of the Indus Valley civilization days. This chapter is dedicated to the first-ever full-fledged civilization in India.

To begin talking about the history of food in India, there is no better starting point than the Indus Valley. The first proper civilization in early India, it dates back approximately to 2600 BC–1700 BC.[3] There was, though, a prolonged pre-Harappan period before this. So, to understand this fully, let us start from the very beginning, when India's geography was nothing like what we know today.

The Geography

Imagine the earth and its landmass as a couple who are constantly breaking and patching up. It all starts with Rodinia, a supercontinent that existed at least 750 million years ago, when all of the earth's landmass was one. Due to certain natural tendencies of the planet, Rodinia broke up into several smaller masses. This period is loosely known as 'pre-Cambrian', or the earliest part of earth's history.[4] (Note, one of the relics from this period exists in India even today and is perhaps the oldest surviving geological feature in the whole world—the Aravalli range.)

About 270 million years ago, these broken pieces of Rodinia began to reassemble and fuse together into a large continent called Pangea. This time, India landed up somewhere between Africa, the Madagascar islands,

Antarctica and Australia. Then, around 175 million years ago, another break led to Pangea splitting into two large continents, Laurasia (consisting of North America, Europe and Asia) and the southern continent called Gondwana, which consisted of Africa, South America, Antarctica, Australia and India (the central Indian Gond tribe gets its name from the word Gondwana).

Centuries passed before India separated from Africa, then from Antarctica and lastly from Madagascar, drifting steadily northwards. It finally collided with the Eurasian plate (the combined landmass of Europe and Asia), which caused the Himalayas to form. It is believed that India is still slowly moving further northwards.[5]

How is this relevant to food in India? This is just to say that even before India became the country that you and I know today, a lot of geological changes had taken place on earth. They have been happening for centuries and will continue to do so in the years to come. So, organically, a lot of cross-continental exchanges had already taken place before large civilizations formed on the continent; therefore, my first question—what is authentically Indian to begin with?

The First People of India

Before defining food, I want to define the Indian people. There are a lot of contradictory theories that attempt to explain how the population was formed in the central and south Asian part of the earth. And interestingly, agriculture has an important role to play here.

Up until the twentieth century, it was believed that India was originally inhabited by aboriginal Stone Age tribes till about 1500 BC (the Stone Age started around 8700 BC, so you can imagine how long this period was).[6] Then, an Indo-European group called the Aryans 'invaded' India with iron weapons, and the Indian civilization was a result of this invasion.

This theory was backed by the Nazis, who felt that the Indo-European language-speaking, light-skinned and blue-eyed Aryans were a group that conquered ancient India and subsequently led to the development of ancient Indian culture. The theory was further reinforced by the British, who justified colonialists as being latter-day Aryans who were here just to civilize the native Indians. However, this was not accepted by Hindutva thinkers, who argued that Indo-European culture, in fact, originated in India first and spread westward from there. The truth is far from these theories, and yet the theories are not entirely wrong.

One of the latest genomic studies of the south and central Indian population reveals something a bit more complex in terms of the genetics that form the original south Asian ancestry. The most striking thing about this population is that there was a lot of genetic diversity found here, perhaps second only to Africa, and this diversity seems to be primarily a result of migration.

After about 6000 BC, the Indian subcontinent mainly consisted of three kinds of people. The first were the south

Asian hunter-gatherers, perhaps the oldest inhabitants of the subcontinent. Then there were (maybe Iranian) agriculturists who migrated from western Asia, possibly bringing with them certain forms of cultivation of wheat, pulses and barley. The last migration was by the Steppe pastoralists, people from around the Volga and Don rivers in Russia (loosely referred to as the 'Aryans'), who migrated towards India, encountering the Indus Valley population. And this mighty mix is what may have formed a group called 'early Indians'.[7]

Role of Agriculture

To understand how cuisine shaped up, I began by looking at how agriculture started, and that led me to Mehrgarh. One of the earliest documented experiments in agriculture can be found in a village at the foot of the Bolan Pass, in current-day Balochistan, Pakistan. Mehrgarh was first discovered in 1976 by archaeologist Jean-François Jarrige,[8] who excavated it with his team.[9] The village and its agricultural practices belonged to around 7000 BC–5500 BC. These practices were considered the foundation for the Indus Valley civilization that was to follow, but not before several hundred years passed.

What the archaeologists found shapes our understanding of how agriculture began in South Asia and how it could have spread. Firstly, the archaeologists discovered agricultural tools such as sickles made of microliths instead of metal, which could have been used to harvest grain. Fossils of seeds such as emmer and einkorn wheat and barley were found.

7

Barley happens to be the most primitive grain mankind has grown on this subcontinent. Besides, there were wild animal remains—wild pig, gazelle, nilgai and blackbuck—pointing to what meats could have been eaten during this time and also the remains of some domesticated animals.[10]

This is probably the first period in the history of India when man turned from hunting and gathering to domesticating animals. Therefore, Mehrgarh is a good example to understand this transition. Thankfully, archaeological findings confirm that they didn't only discover wild grains, seeds and animals, but also some domesticated foods. The remains indicate that some of the plants and animals seem to have undergone a process of domestication, if not full domestication, perhaps making the people of Mehrgarh the first agriculturists of South Asia.[11] Domesticated animals included the sheep, goat, water buffalo and the indigenous zebu cattle; in fact, the last two accounted for more than half of the animal remains found here, the rest being wild animals, as observed by the archaeologist and zoologist R.H. Meadow.[12]

For most early civilizations, such transitions were gradual and happened over centuries, after which man moved from his meat gathering stage to agriculture—though in some civilizations, people went back from farming to hunting, as in the Sahara grasslands, as soon as the climate permitted them to do so. But, of course, they eventually reverted to farming.

In spite of all these findings, it is still too ambitious to say that agriculture in South Asia was solely a Mehrgarh phenomenon, because similar forms of early agricultural remains have been found in other regions in the subcontinent. In Lahuradewa in the upper Ganges, wild rice cultivation can be traced back to around 7000 BC. And there are such other remains that have been found in regions in Gujarat, Rajasthan, the Malwa plateau in Madhya Pradesh, in the Vindhyas, in Kashmir and in the Swat Valley, although these were from much after the Mehrgarh period. But nowhere do we see Indus Valley staples like wheat and barley as we do in Mehrgarh. Mehrgarh domesticated wild barley, followed by wheat. Since it was in the heart of Balochistan, wheat could have come from the Middle Eastern agriculturists, considering this region was a busy Indo-Iranian route.[13] As with the Indus Valley civilization or any other era of Indian history, Mehrgarh too developed in stages and archaeologists also found fire pits with charred stones, associated with one of its later stages. They also found remains of oval-shaped stones and interestingly, even today, in that same region in Pakistan, one can find bread made on heated oval stones.

The village of Mehrgarh gradually paved the way for the Indus Valley civilization to flourish. Somewhere between 2600 BC and 2000 BC, Mehrgarh started being abandoned for bigger centres that may have been precursors to the Indus cities such as Hakra, Kot Diji, Amri, Nal and Ahar.

The Indus Valley Civilization

The Indus Valley civilization was one of the four most important civilizations that flourished in the cradle of fertile river valleys. Together with the Egyptian, Mesopotamian and Yellow River valleys, it makes up the 'old world'. Though the four civilizations did not exist at the same time, they have a lot in common.

In 1856, when the Lahore–Multan railway lines were being constructed in India, archaeologists came across remains of the lost city of Harappa. At this point not much was done about the discovery. It was only in 1921, after a gap of more than half a century, that in-depth excavations led by Sir John Marshall, then director-general of the Archaeological Survey of India, and his team began.[14] Marshall and his team dug up and studied the remains to understand how the Harappans lived and how widespread the Indus Valley civilization was. Excavations took place in Harappa (Punjab), Mohenjo-Daro (Sind) and many smaller sites such as Kot Diji (Sind), Kalibangan (Rajasthan), Rupar (Punjab), Rakhigarhi, Banawali, Mitathal (Haryana), Lothal, Dholavira, Surkotada (Gujarat) and Ganweriwala (Bahawalpur). Some scholars like to call this civilization the Indus–Saraswati civilization as settlements were found around the Ghaggar (Saraswati) river basin too. The civilization whose remains archaeologists first found was different from the one at Mehrgarh, and so they understood that it belonged to a much later period in Indian history. The Indus Valley civilization came about during the Bronze Age, which came after the Stone Age and before the Iron Age. This means copper alloys were among the most important materials to be discovered and used during this period in history. The Indus people had access to fire for cooking, wheels to move around and work in the fields, and basic agricultural know-how. But refined iron tools had not been invented yet. It was kind of like waiting for the next iPhone, only it took centuries!

The excavations throw light on a sophisticated administration and well-defined way of life. There were discoveries of hidden assembly halls, citadels, perhaps an educational institution and, most importantly for this chapter, the remains of what could have been large granaries used to store grains. The granary structure and the seeds are the biggest proof of the Indus people being agriculturalists. It was perhaps also the first time in the history of India that man was capable of generating sufficient food for his community, even for those who may not have been primarily engaged in agriculture or hunting.

We already know that Mehrgarh had begun domesticating plants and animals, and the Indus Valley population took this a step further. The earlier populations were still hunters and gatherers who were dabbling in agriculture. We understand this from the site of Bagor, one of the best-preserved archaeological sites in India, located on the left bank of the Kothari river in Bhilwara district of Rajasthan. The excavations here included tools, microliths and animal remains, which were found at different levels, revealing a civilization that was based on a combination of hunting-gathering and herding and that evolved over a large period of time.[15] The mature Harappan period saw sophisticated farmers whose agricultural know-how is surprisingly not very different from what we understand about farming today.

The upper layers of the Harappan excavations included findings such as terracotta ploughs, stone blades for harvesting, bull seals to indicate the animals' contribution to farming, and wooden, copper and bronze tools that may have been used in the fields.

Besides using rudimentary tools, the Indus people had developed mature crop systems, which shows their knowledge of crop patterns and seasonality. Some researchers speculate the presence of Harappan astronomers who observed the sky and nature, and evidence of this lies in their rock art that displays symbols which prove that they observed the movements of the sun, moon, stars and sky. The excavation of the 'calendar stone' in Mohenjo-Daro shows that it was necessary for the Indus Valley people to understand agricultural patterns and seasons.

We know that the inhabitants of the Indus Valley mainly grew rabi crops that were sown in winter and harvested in spring. In certain periods, they practised intercropping too; pulses grew with cereals, and they used cattle, goat and sheep manure as fertilizers.

Furrows found in many Harappan sites further attest to their knowledge of agriculture. In Kalibangan, researchers discovered cross-furrows, which means that in one direction they sowed one crop, and another cereal or pulses were planted at a 90-degree angle to enable intercropping.

Since the Kalibangan settlement was on semi-arid land, rainfall was below 250 mm per annum and there were long gaps between rainy days. Agriculture would not have been easy, as the water was saline and potable water was scarce. But so far, there isn't any direct evidence of irrigation. The people of the Indus Valley civilization may have built water diversion schemes, used fertile alluvial soil left by the rivers after the flood season, harvested rain and used fish traps to farm fishes. In fact, at Dholavira they harvested flash floods and rainwater. They had large rock-cut reservoirs, wells and stone drains that would have been used to save water for agriculture, drinking, household and industrial use. Besides, annual flooding of the Indus brought down rich silt, making irrigated lands fertile.

During the early Indus period, agriculture may not have been just an economic activity, but also a social one; especially the threshing floor, which would have been an interesting place for people to mingle. Crop-processing stages included harvesting, threshing, winnowing by wind and shaking of the grain, sieving, pounding and grinding.

As the period ripened, agriculture gained momentum and became a serious vocation. Proof of this can be seen in the granaries of the Indus Valley period. Some archaeologists like to call them 'great halls' instead of granaries, as no proof of grain storage containers or clay sealings was found here.[16] Conversely, some scholars felt that the absence of storage containers does not prove that the 'halls' are not granaries because grain could have been piled in heaps on the floor or in cotton or leather sacks.

A study of these structures gives us a peek into Indus Valley life. They showed various levels of food processing and the presence of authority for distribution. The society may have had people labouring in the fields and granaries, working in non-food-producing vocations. There was perhaps an overarching authority to look into the assimilation of resources available for people to use in the community since standardization of tools and pottery has been observed throughout the settlements, pointing at the existence of a central authority among the various Indus Valley sites.

The sites also reveal steady domestication of animals, and of vegetable and other produce at the same time as it was happening in other ancient civilizations. This points to multiple trade routes connecting them to an outer world and an exchange of knowledge on harvesting and seeding.

For example, sugarcane, which was thought of as native to India, was first domesticated by Me Lenesians in New Guinea (they may have also domesticated the banana, although a separate species may have been independently domesticated in India). Similarly, rice and pigs were first domesticated in China.[17] Sesame[18] and cotton[19] appear to have been first cultivated in India. Domestication of cows, too, happened first in India, while separately it also appears to have taken place in the Middle East during a similar period.

According to archaeologist Steven Weber,

No more than 70 sites in all of South Asia dating to earlier than 1000 BC have yielded plant remains of some form. These help us understand the human-plant interrelationship. Similarities in pottery, weights and seals are strong evidence for a shared ideology and suggest the existence of an administrative system to oversee the manufacturing and distribution of goods.[20]

It is also speculated that clay tags were used to identify ownership of crops before they were bundled and transported to granaries from the threshing floor. One reading is that the Indus symbols indicates a set of visuals referring to crops and share of agriculture—how much belonged to God, the state, the city, the landowner or the farmer. But these are just a few of the thousand archaeological assumptions made about the civilization. By the time the Harappan period ended, the Indian subcontinent was a wholesome agricultural community.

Food in the Indus Valley

In June 2016, I read about one of the most interesting pieces of research about the Harappan culinary world. It was in an article published by the BBC about a project undertaken by archaeologists Arunima Kashyap and Steve Weber of Vancouver's Washington State University in 2010, trying to find clues to the earliest foods of the Indian subcontinent.[21] The duo conducted a starch analysis of the molecules gathered from the utensils and tools found on the excavation site in Farmana—south-east of the largest Harappan city of Rakhigarhi. They used this method to determine what the Harappans ate during the peak years of their civilization from 2500 BC to 1800 BC.[22]

Molecules of starch were extracted from pots, pans, stone tools and the dental enamel of both humans and animal fossils, since animals were often fed leftovers. At the end of this research, what Kashyap and Weber discovered was surprising, and yet not too shocking.

We have established that during the early Harappan period, approximately from 3300 BC to 2600 BC, the Harappans dabbled in wheat and barley. They ate them whole or powdered (mainly groats and roughage), and their bread was coarse. Kashyap and Weber's research brought to the fore a picture of a more nuanced meal which they may have been eating. Their research pointed to the possibility of eggplant, turmeric and ginger (maybe even clove), and they came up with a rough recipe, titled 'proto curry', or what may have been the very first curry of the subcontinent, over 4,000 years ago.

The research indicates that the people of ancient Farmana possibly cooked in and ate off terracotta vessels or unbaked earthen pots. They fed the leftovers of their food to the cattle (a practice seen in rural India even today). This is why similar starch molecules were discovered in the animals' dental fossils too.

As the transition from a village-based society to an urban one took place, the subsistence base broadened, from foods that had been eaten for thousands of years, such as wild game, fish and wild plants, to include new food resources, such as domestic sheep, goat, cattle and domesticated grains.

Harappans were eating everything from pulses (green peas and chickpeas), lentils, grams (green and black) and field beans to okra, mustard greens, coriander, and fruits such as the banana, date, jujube, fig, mango, sugarcane and pomegranate. But these looked nothing like our hyper-domesticated, perfect crops. The Harappans even used sesame, flax and linseed for oil. The plants found at both rural and urban sites were being grown to yield grain for the people and straw for the animals. However, there is a dearth of evidence to substantiate these claims.

In the Mehrgarh period, food production was a predominantly South Asian phenomenon; but in the Indus Valley civilization, trade became a part of their lives too. Especially trade with Mesopotamia. This is verified from the recovery of Harappan-style seals, beads and weights found in Mesopotamia, confirming the possibility of the interconnection between these two civilizations via Iran or via their maritime routes (Harappan weights and measures were a standard across the region.)

While the above discussed grains were the sustenance crops of the Indus Valley during the mature period, it was only around 2000 BC that jowar made an appearance here from eastern Africa. Many researchers describe it as the 'first-ever green revolution'. Since millets do not require dense alluvial soil (like the Nile river belt) to grow and are less fussy about water, they spread quickly and grow well in the Indian terrain. Apart from jowar, seed residues of kodo, sanwa and ragi (foxtail millet) can be found during the most mature period.

An interesting point of discussion is whether the Indus Valley people used spices and salt. While some researchers have found evidence of Indian spices such as cumin and clove from the most mature phase of the civilization, some others say that the Indus people ate food without any kind of seasoning except salt. The salt may have come from the salt pans of Dholavira or the Rann of Kutch. Dholavira is believed to have been once connected to the Arabian Sea by a water channel, an arm of the sea, though no evidence of such a waterway has been found.

There was heavy reliance on dairy during this period. However, it wasn't as prominent as it became in the upcoming Vedic society. Those who have studied the Indus diet claim that the people drank goat, sheep and cow milk and ate their meat too.[23] For the Indus Valley civilization, the drawing of animal motifs was a popular hobby, from the earliest to the most mature phase. And based on their depictions, archaeologists and archaeozoologists have tried to understand which animals may have been a part of their environment (elephant, camel, dog, cat, rhinoceros), which may have been eaten as game meat (fowl, nilgai, stag, spotted deer, sambar deer, hog deer) and which may have simply been domesticated (oxen, zebu cattle, buffalo, goat, pig, sheep, onager).

From the scale of animal remains and bones found in Indus Valley sites, it is evident that animals were reared extensively.

Obviously, the Indus Valley did not have had full-fledged cheese production capabilities. Scholars suspect the existence of milk products such as butter, clarified butter, curd and cottage cheese in the most mature periods.[24]

One food item that was available extensively in the Indus Valley was fish. Since the entire civilization was supported by a river and its four tributaries (Jhelum, Chenab, Sutlej and Ravi), fish and fisheries may have played an important role in the diet of the people.

The Indus Delta provided a diverse environment of tidal channels, mudflats and mangrove swamps. It had rivers, lakes, swamps and canals that were rich with fish and other marine life. Archaeological discoveries found the remains of a variety of fish including sciaenidae or drums, rohu, catla, mori, masheer, herring, shad, knife fish, feather fish, moli, freshwater shark, snakeheads, catfish, spiny eel, mullet, flounders, turbot, sole, parrot fish, stingray, eagle ray, terrapin, Bombay duck, flathead and sea bass.

It is interesting to note the remarkable connection between the fish industry of those times and what we see today. As with the other aspects of Indus life, our understanding of their fishing communities is based on the motifs found on pottery and ceramics, and the discovery of fish hooks (mostly in copper and bronze). It can be seen that the method of the fishermen from the coastal sites of Kutch is not too different from those in Pakistan even today, like the use of specific curved metal (copper) knives, net weirs or throw-nets.

Leftovers of pottery found during the excavations also lend an interesting view of how the Indus people ate. Archaeologists have found storage jars, offering stands (similar to the modern-day cake stand), cups with finger holders, querns, cooking pots and bowls of all sizes, depicting the portion sizes they may have been cooking or eating. Then there are the rare pottery items with a vent to release whey, which archaeologists imagine may have been used to make something like cottage cheese, and thatched mud ovens that were used to roast barley.

There was definitely a system of eating curry with bread, as we have found separate bowls for liquid (curry) and solid (bread) foods. Plates with rims may have been used to knead flour. Mortars and pestles were also excavated, but those could have been used to grind pigments into powder and not necessarily for food. Most of these were in materials such as terracotta, bronze, stone, tin and alloy, and, in small proportions, lead, silver, and gold.

Where Did the Indus Valley People Go?

Now that we have established who the Indus people were, what they grew, and how they cooked and ate, it is important to understand what the next step for the Indian kitchen was—where did the Indus Valley people go, and who came after them?

Availability of food and an increase in population were among the major reasons behind smaller Indus sites becoming into larger ones, often far away from each other.

Small settlemets slowly turned into villages, then into towns and finally into cities. At its peak, one of the civilization's most populous cities, Harappa, became a fully developed city complex, housing a population of over 35,000.[25]

Then, around 1900 BC, the Indus Valley region went through a series of climatic changes and the cities started to perish. Slow changes in river patterns, the resultant floods and sedimentation, crop failure and deforestation were some of the major reasons, overpopulation being another, of the civilization eroding.

Looking at the civilization's ruins, scholars have noticed signs of overcrowded cities, where houses were built on top of each other. At one point, settlements began to be abandoned. Gradual cultural, political and trade collapse came next. Mesopotamia, with whom the civilization had a major trade relationship, was going through a huge political change too. Trade networks may have weakened, and this would have further had an impact on Indus cities, leading to their disintegration.

2

THE IMPACT OF RELIGION

I'm a regular at scrolling the brightest of health and wellness content there is—blogs, vlogs, websites . . . hello, Hemsley + Hemsley, mindbodygreen, Goop, Brit + Co. I spend a large part of my day reading about things like adaptogens, reishi mushrooms and collagen ramen, and what they do for your gut, body, nails, hair and, well, mostly just skin. Sometimes I dedicate a full hour to finding the perfect green smoothie . . . you don't want me to get started on that nut butter, leaf and fruit ratio that I have cracked.

So, while on this research project, as I deep-dived into the Vedic kitchen, I couldn't be more convinced that what Western media have glorified as superfoods in recent times mostly came right out of an Indian kitchen centuries ago. What I'm eating is exactly what they ate in the early Vedic period, of course in a more rustic form. This feels especially so when I mix my raw honey with nut mylk, and then all of that with some barley flakes and ashwagandha for breakfast.

I've been observing the West's obsession with turmeric powder, ginger tea, lemon shots, jackfruit 'meat', ghee and seed oil. Barring avocado toast, many of these glam food seem to have made an appearance in ancient Vedic wisdom. Now, I'm not trying to patronize the ancient Indian way of eating, but am pointing out that science and spirituality support how well early Indians ate as far back as 1500 BC.

For me, the study of mainstream religion's impact on Indian cuisine begins with the rise of Vedic society. In Hinduism, food emerges as something sacred. It is almost one with the soul. It was fed to the belly of a fire in religious rituals (ghee to the havan), it is cosmic (man equated food with Brahman), and it was considered the breath of life or what the ancient scriptures called 'prana'.

Rig Veda (Hymn 187)[1]
Now I shall praise food, the support and power of the great . . .
O sweet food, honeyed food, we have chosen you: for us be a helper.
Draw near to us, food – kindly with your kindly help Joy itself, not to be despised, a very kind companion without duplicity.
These juices of yours, food, are dispersed throughout the realms, adjoined to heaven like the winds.
These [juices] are those that yield you, O food, and they also are part of you, sweetest food.
Those who receive the sweetness of your juices press

forward like strong-necked [bulls]
On you, food, is the mind of the great gods set.
A deed was done at your signal; he smashed the serpent
with your help.
When yonder dawning light of the mountains has come,
O food,
Then you should also come here to us, honeyed food, fit
for our portion.
When we bite off a full share of the waters and plants,
O you friend of the winds – become just the fat.
When we take a share of you when mixed with milk or
mixed with grain, O Soma,
O you friend of the winds, become just the fat.
Become the gruel, O plant, the fat, the steaming suet
O you friend of the winds – become just the fat
We have sweetened you with words, O food, as cows' milk
does the oblations
You as feasting companions for the gods, you as feasting
companions for us.

Hints of what to eat, when to eat and how to eat are everywhere. In the Ramayana's description of honey extraction and distillations to food references in Upanishads (from earth herbs, from herbs food, from food seed, from seed man; man, thus, consists of the essence of food—Taittiriya Upanishad) and in the Bhagwad Gita (All beings come into existence from food. Food comes from rains. Rain originates from the performance of sacrifices. And sacrifice is born out of doing prescribed duties—3:14) alike.[2]

The scriptures, texts, hymns and shlokas are strewn with mentions of foods like milk, honey, fruits, soma, and the names of plants and grains. And since the scriptures are varied and from eras spanning thousands of years, a good starting point for me to understand how religion impacted Indian cuisine was the Vedic period, falling roughly between 1500 BC and 500 BC.[3]

The Vedic period was the time when trickles of religious ideologies and texts first appeared on the Indian subcontinent. And foremost among these were the Vedas, the oldest of Sanskrit literature. The period gets its name from the works that were revealed/composed during this time, in case you haven't caught that yet. My surname too has a connection, but that's a story for another time.

There are four Vedas in all—the *Rig Veda*, the *Yajur Veda*, the *Sama Veda* and the *Atharva Veda*. Fortunately for us, they are chock-full of edible references. The ample food citations I found in their English translations help us understand this period better, giving us insight into what food was like in the Indian subcontinent during the period of history when the texts were composed.

The *Rig Veda* came into being sometime between 1700 BC and 1100 BC.[4] Interestingly, the dates overlap with some of the phases of the Indus Valley civilization, and so you will spot many similarities between the Vedic and Valley kitchens. For me, one of the biggest cues is that the *Rig Veda* doesn't mention iron as a material at all, and we do not see iron remains in Indus valley sites. If prehistory is neatly divided into materials and their usage, this is clear proof that both these periods were pre-Iron Age. In both periods, people mainly relied on clay, stone or bronze. Iron, though, is mentioned sparingly in the last of the four books, the *Atharva Veda*, which was composed in the later part of the Vedic period.[5]

The second cue lies in the fact that both these periods are associated with rivers that were at the centre of development. While the Indus Valley civilization gets its name from the river Indus, the *Rig Veda* talks about a certain 'great river'. Not only does it have forty-five dedicated verses about this natural body of water, no other geographical feature is mentioned with as much fervour as this river, which is also called the 'inspirer of hymns', further suggesting that this scripture was perhaps composed on its banks. (Scholars suspect this river to be the Saraswati, and not the main Indus; as described in Chapter 1, plenty of Indus settlements were found on the banks of the Saraswati too.) In the Brahmanas, there is a mention of the disappearance of this mighty river into a desert. A similar fate befell the Indus Valley civilization, researchers say: they have talked of the Indus river drying up, leading to its collapse.

The parallels make it hard to ignore the possibility that they are all referring to the same period and people. There were differences too, though. For example, the later Harappan civilization was essentially an urban one, while Rig Vedic society was mainly agricultural, pastoral and philosophical. Besides, the *Rig Veda* nowhere mentions the municipal order that the Harappans were obsessed with. But then again, the *Rig Veda* is a religious book, so why would it talk about civics?

So, could the two civilizations have been the same, after all? My understanding is that it is safe to assume that, like Bandra West, perhaps the Indus society too was a multi-ethnic society, and the Vedic people were a part of that society, like the foreigners you'll see savouring moringa smoothies post a yogalates class.

One of the main grains mentioned in the *Rig Veda* is the same one that we discussed in the context of the earlier Harappan civilization—barley.[6] In the previous chapter, we saw that there is very little information on how the Indus people ate barley. We only know that barley was found in excavations and pottery residues. But the Vedas go so far as to refer to the different ways of eating barley. The *Rig Veda* itself mentions grinding, forming cakes out of it, frying it in fat, eating it dried or ground, and mixing it with milk and curd.[7] There were as many ways to eat barley back then as there are ways to eat cauliflower today. Except for turning it into pizza.

The *Rig Veda* is where we find mentions of what was perhaps the first Indian mithai too. It was a dish called apupa, which not only sounds like malpua, but was also made in a similar way.[8] My kale juice-slurping millennial self is pleased to report that the first-ever Indian mithai wasn't a milk-dripping, sugar-loaded carb ball, but a high-on-minerals and fibre-loaded, sugar-free crêpe. Hello, barley flour pancakes! Apupa were essentially small flat rounds made out of barley flour, either deep-fried in ghee or boiled and served with drizzles of honey. This helps us understand one of the ways in which barley—the most common grains during the Vedic period—was used at that time. The *Rig Veda* also tells us that honey was the most common sweetener back then.

Over time the apupas may have changed character, as in later literature we find them to be made out of wheat flour, milk, clarified butter and sugar, with spices such as cardamom, pepper and ginger added to the batter.[9] Various cultural influences modified the recipe, and apupas took the form of pupalika, a small cake of rice or wheat flour fried in ghee with jaggery, and may have also developed into various versions of the malpua, including the one made with eggs and mawa, popularized by the Islamic court. Today, malpua is a festive treat made during festivals like Holi, Diwali and Ramadan, and in different parts of the subcontinent they are called by different names: amalu in Odisha, pithey in West Bengal, marpa in Nepal.

Food in the Vedas progresses as we move to the subsequent scriptures. In the second and the third Vedas, there are mentions of more evolved Indian dishes. The *Yajur Veda* has a prayer that gives insight into the importance of food and sustenance for the people of this period.

May for me prosper, through the yajna, milk, sap, ghee, honey, eating and drinking at the common table, ploughing, rains, conquest, victory, wealth, riches. May for me prosper, through the yajna, low-grade food, freedom from hunger, rice, barley, sesame, kidney beans, vetches, wheat, lentils, millets, panicum grains and wild rice. May for me prosper, through the yajna, trees, plants, that which grows in ploughed land, and that which grows in unploughed land.

It is interesting to note that in all the four Vedas, cattle played an important role, starting from the *Rig Veda*, which has about 700 verses mentioning the cow as a symbol of bounty (buffalo and goat also find mentions). If you are a new vegan, you won't be too pleased to hear that Ayurvedic texts put dairy in a unique food category and claim it has nutritional value like no other food.[10] The Vedas contain references to a dish or an ingredient called dadhi (present-day dahi), which was eaten plain or with whole grains. I imagine this to taste like my curd and whole-grain breakfast bowl, drizzled with honey. Perhaps they had the culinary genius to add a few cubes of fresh fruit to this too.

The Vedas also mention a dish where dahi was mixed with soma and folded into fresh milk to make a drink (lassi), and shikarini, the modern-day shrikhand, made of strained curd, sugar and fragrant herbs—not too different from how it is made today. Buttermilk existed, and so did a dish called karambha, which I equate to a modern-day grain bowl—milk turned into curd and mixed with honey and barley.

Ayurveda has always forbidden the curdling of milk, but research points to primitive communities curdling milk by introducing green leaves to it and not lemon juice. The use of lemon juice to curdle milk began only around 800 BC, with the *Yajur Veda,* and maybe even the lemons came then too.[11]

Ayurvedic texts also mention the usage of bovine colostrum. Known as posu in Konkani, ginna in Kannada, kharvas in Marathi, cheek in Hindi, bari in Gujarati and kadambu paal in Tamil, this is made of the milk of a lactating cow available only for 3 or 4 days and is served as milky squares, usually steamed. This has been mentioned in the Vedic texts.

The Vedas also mention dadhanvat, which food historians roughly translate to mean cheese.[12] The dish was prepared by adding curd into boiled milk, splitting it into a fatty portion called amiksa, and a thin liquid or whey, known as vajina.

While there aren't enough texts proving that dairy products such as clarified butter and other fats were in use in the Indus Valley, there is ample mention of them in the Vedic texts. Ghee was used copiously by the higher castes, and it was fed to the sacred fire during rituals, mixed with flour. Milk, an important part of the Vedic diet, was consumed in raw, boiled and cooked form.

An interesting dish that comes to the fore in the Vedas, something we will find in other books too, is a porridge called odana.[13] And as we move from the *Rig Veda* to the *Atharva Veda*, its preparation becomes more and more refined. Odana, a goop made of milk and barley, is bestowed with the divine power of making the eater experience heaven in a bite, the books say. Much like a well-made tiramisu, I say.

There are different versions of milk pudding that pop up in the Vedic texts. The rishi Upamanyu in the *Rig Veda* talks about his mother giving him a cake called pistam (flour ball), while he requests her for ksirodah (a rice pudding). His tapasya earns him a blessing from the gods, who promise him eternal youth and an ocean of milk pudding or 'ksirodah sagarah'.

There are mentions of other kinds of rice-based dishes, like dadhyodana, in which curd is mixed with rice. I imagine this to taste like a cooling bowl of thayir sadam. Tamil Iyengars' curd-rice is called dhadhiyodhanam to this day. In a rice dish called tilaudana, nutty sesame seeds are added; ghrtaudana has rice mashed with ghee; mudgaudana contains beans; and mamsaudana has meat in it.[14]

For grains, the Vedas start with barley, slowly moving towards rice, just as we have seen in the Indus Valley too. Mind you, these changes took place over hundreds of years. Rice takes centre stage in later Vedic texts, post the composition of the *Rig Veda*. There is mention of different varieties of rice in the *Yajur Veda* and in the Brahmanas, and there appears to be as many varieties as we would find in an aisle at Foodhall. Black rice, check; short-grain rice, check; red rice, check; white rice, check; wild rice, check too. These were used to make dishes like parivapa, which was rice fried in fat; purodasa, a rice cake; laja, puffed rice; and prthuka, beaten rice.

Contrary to what modern-day Hindutva philosophy would have us believe, eating beef was quotidian, just as it was during the Harappan civilization. Vedic texts confirm the slaughtering of cattle for sacrificial rituals. This wasn't an everyday affair, but was done to feed guests of importance. Mainly, the meat of a barren cow was eaten during feasts like weddings. Later, around 1000 BC, as agriculture gained momentum, religious texts began preaching against eating meat, especially beef, which became a taboo as the cow became too valuable to be slaughtered.[15]

Fruits and vegetables too find ample representation in the Vedas and are not too different from those mentioned in Chapter 1. There is mention of jujube, bael, dates, Indian gooseberry, cucumber, lotus stalks, edible roots, bottle gourd, bitter gourd and water chestnut.[16] Now, if only they had some miso and tofu, they could make themselves an epic Japanese dinner.

A fruit which occupies a central place in ancient scriptures is the mango. It's not just the Jains of Malabar Hill who vie to be the first to get their hands on a sweet-smelling mango when the season begins; this Indian fruit has been the apple of the eye (inappropriate choice of idiom) since early times. Sometimes referred to as amara or amra phal in the Indian subcontinent, mango first finds mention in the *Satapatha Brahmana* (a prose text describing Vedic rituals, history and mythology associated with the *Yajur Veda*).[17] It was historically one of the most relished indigenous fruits, and continues to be so.

The similarity between some Indian scriptures and my Instagram feed in the summer is that we both can't stop talking about mangoes. Valmiki's Ramayana mentions it, and the Vedic Cupid Kamadeva, or Kama, is known to shoot arrows of mango blossoms at gods and humans. Kalidasa's play *Shakuntala* too mentions this.

Palaeobotanical research points to the Indo-Burma-Malay region as the place where the mango originated.[18] From there it moved to China, to the Philippines, and to other regions of

South-East Asia and the rest of the world. The fruit caught the attention of early foreign travellers to the subcontinent, like Xuanzang (Hsüan-tsang), Ibn-Haukul, Ibn-Battuta and Ludovici di Varthema. And it was Hsüan-tsang, a Chinese Buddhist monk who travelled to India in the seventh century and described the interaction between the practices of Chinese Buddhism and Indian Buddhism, who first brought the Indian mango to the notice of people outside India. The mango holds a special place in Buddhism too, where the mango tree is mentioned several times in religious texts.[19] The Portuguese, fascinated by the juicy yellow fruit on their arrival in Kerala, introduced vegetative propagation methods so the fruit could reach the rest of the world.

Another fruit that finds mention in both Hinduism and Buddhism is amalaki, or the predecessor of the amla. There are several religious references that confirm its origin in the Indian subcontinent. Once such is a story about the goddesses Parvati and Lakshmi. When they wept, their tears fell to the earth and thus the amalaki plant germinated. Since then, the leaves of the tree have been considered sacred and are used in the worship of the gods Shiva and Vishnu. Hindus believe that the god Krishna resides in an amla plant, while Sikhs believe their gurus rested under it. The amla finds ample representation in the *Atharva Veda* (*Charaka Samhita*) too. The Puranas say that washing hair with its juice rids one of all sins.

The Puranas mention other fruits, like badari (maybe the same as Indian jujube) and bilva (or bael), which don't have much contemporary usage. I can confirm though that these fruits can be sourced even now at local vegetable markets in cities, often sold by tribals. I convert bael into a refreshing sherbet come summer, and am sipping it as I type these words. Another indigenous fruit that can be traced back to this period is the Indian lemon, known as jambhila. Research confirms that the earliest mentions of citrus can be found in the *Vajasaneyi Samhita*, which was part of the *Yajur Veda*, as early as the eighth century BC. Several botanical researchers point to the heirloom citrus species as having originated in the south-eastern foothills of the Himalayas, specifically in the eastern part of Assam (the Khasi hills), northern Myanmar and western Yunnan in China, and later spread to different parts of the world. Today, the lemon is used in kitchens almost all over India.

For me, the *Yajur Veda* is a treasure trove for understanding the Vedic kitchen, which wasn't too different from an average rural Indian kitchen. Imagine clay pots filled with urad, mung and masoor dal that have been farmed or were purchased from the local markets.

One of my most fascinating discoveries is the mention of the word 'tila' in the ancient scriptures. It means til, or sesame in English. The importance of sesame seeds is mentioned in the *Atharva Veda* too. Tila is probably one of the earliest oilseeds known to mankind, and historians believe that the word 'taila', and subsequently the word 'tel', may have been derived from it.[20]

A spice often mentioned in the Vedas is rajika, a species of black mustard grown in the Indus Valley. One of its varieties is called baja in the *Atharva Veda*. Hymns describe the baja—or pinga, it's variant—as a strong-smelling herb that chases demons away.

Honey was probably the earliest sweetener, with the references to it dating back to the *Rig Veda*.[21] The text mentions in detail how it was collected from two kinds of bees: the big one known as 'arangara' and the small one as 'saragha'. The latter's honey was considered better than the former's, and was used to sweeten apupas. Take a moment to appreciate this: the earliest Indian enjoyed a plate of honey-drizzled pancakes, gluten- and sugar-free ones at that.

The subcontinent may also have introduced sugar to the world, and it is then no wonder that we are a country obsessed with all things sweet. The Vedic texts support that sugar existed even during that period. In fact, historians claim that the very word is a derivative of the Sanskrit word 'sarkara'; however, the word denoting sugar in the Vedas is iksu (*Atharva Veda*).[22] Sugar may have gradually replaced honey as a sweetener. A dessert named mandaka, a large wheat bread stuffed with sweet lentil paste, was sweetened with sugar. I imagine this to taste like puran poli, except that puran poli is sweetened with jaggery. People in Vedic times also made payasa, rice cooked with thickened milk and sugar; maybe payasa was the predecessor of payasam.

One ingredient mentioned several times throughout the Vedas is soma, and this needs a book of its own. Soma seems to have been considered a spiritual drink. In one of the chapters in the *Rig Veda*, the ninth mandala is also called the Soma mandala, with 114 hymns devoted to 'soma pavamana' or the 'purifying drink'.[23]

Soma has been revered as a sacred potion used in Vedic religion.[24] An interesting point to note here is the similarity between Vedic and Iranian rituals concerning soma. Just like the fire sacrifices, soma too finds mention in Avestan literature, only, here it's called haoma. Both the Avestan haoma and the Sanskrit soma are derived from the proto-Indo-Iranian word 'sauma', the linguistic root of the word being 'haoma', roughly translating to 'pressing' or 'pounding'.

In the *Rig Veda*, the composer refers freely to soma as a plant, and the Veda talks about its juice and the process of its preparation. It is believed to have a bitter-sour taste and is thought to be immensely beneficial for physical and spiritual health. Although a single plant referred to as soma could have existed in a certain time, place and period in history, it is mostly understood to be a number of sacred plants. For example, the *Atharva Veda* specifically mentions some plants from which the best soma could be extracted. They include—ahem—marijuana, barley and darbha (kusha or durva).[25] Similarly, different types of somas are mentioned in the other Vedas too. However, there is a consensus that soma was mainly found in the Himalayas. Vedic literature experts have come to the conclusion that perhaps soma wasn't derived from a single plant.

While soma is mainly mentioned in tangible terms, it also becomes a bit abstract at times. For example, in one instance the *Rig Veda* refers to soma to mean Himalayan water; in another place the book describes soma as a plant growing near a waterbody and releasing a milk-coloured juice upon crushing. There is also a suggestion for soma to be consumed with milk and curd.[26] Sushruta (an ancient Ayurvedic practitioner and author of the *Compendium of Susruta*, part of the *Atharva Veda*) mentions twenty-four types of soma plants, mainly found in the Himalayas near waterbodies.

Soma was also connected to the practice of alchemy, and in the *Rig Veda* there is a mention of preparing it with gold and possibly with lapis lazuli, seashells and pearls.[27] Finding a single specific soma plant is, therefore, impossible. Interestingly, Vedic scholars say that soma was also described as a secretion in the brain that occurred from spiritual practices such as yoga, pranayama, mantra and meditation. Soma, at the yogic level, refers to the opening of a chakra, leading to a release of bliss throughout the body.

A good idea about what produce was like during the Vedic period can also be had by looking at Ayurvedic texts. Ayurveda is a system of medicine with its roots in the *Atharva Veda*. The popular explanation of how Ayurveda came into being is mentioned in the great Indian physician Sushruta's *Sushruta Samhita* (the Mahabharata mentions Sushruta as a son of the sage Vishvamitra). He prepared the foundational texts of Ayurveda, alongside the *Charaka Samhita* and the *Bhela Samhita*. Together these books mention several food items that helped me understand what food habits and availability of resources were like during the later Vedic period.

At a Himalayan mountain retreat one winter, as I sat in the dappled sunlight chugging a milky concoction of full-fat dairy sprinkled with dry ginger powder and turmeric, I realized how the wisdom of this concoction had been stored in Ayurvedic texts for centuries. Seasons and food play an important role in human health, as mentioned across texts. Which means, during this phase of Indian history, man had a deep understanding of how to work in accordance with both the bounties and vagaries of nature.

Ayurvedic texts classify Indian weather into six different seasons, namely vasanta ritu (spring), grishma ritu (summer), varsha ritu (monsoon), sharad ritu (autumn), hemanta ritu (fall winter) and shishira ritu (winter), and they talk about the foods to be had and the foods that are forbidden during these periods.[28] For example, during hemanta, one could savour the sour and salted juices from the meat of dominantly fatty and aquatic animals, and also the meat of burrow-dwelling animals; one could regularly consume milk products, cane sugar, fats, oil, rice and hot water. In the rainy season too, the diet was to be predominantly sour, salted and fatty; one could eat barley, wheat and rice, along with wild meats and soups. Garlic was suggested for the treatment of heart disease and arthritis.

Shockingly, earlier Ayurveda recommends alcohol, wine, and other types of fermented liquor, mixed with honey and sometimes even rainwater.[29] Says one Ayurvedic text:

One should always drink the best wine, along with various suitable fruit, some green vegetables, salted and seasonal food items, roasted meat of terrestrial, aquatic and flying animals and birds . . . Wine is like nectar for that who drinks according to prescribed method, in proper quantity, in proper time, with wholesome food . . . on the contrary it acts like poison for those who indulge in drinking unwholesome wine . . . observing rough regimens.

Game meat was mentioned often, like that of the peacock, swan, rhinoceros, grey partridge, parrot, sparrow, hare, tortoise; as well as conventional meats such as goat, sheep, pork and beef. Susruta went on to explain in detail the quality of fish residing in ponds, lakes, streams and rivers, and how the Ayurvedic diet advised consuming small fish varieties over larger ones as they are easier to digest, provide instant energy and pacify all the three doshas.[31]

Later, as vegetarianism took over in the subcontinent due to the advent of Jainism and changes in Hinduism, new dietary rules changed the face of Ayurveda too. This modified way is more or less how this form of medicine is practised even today.

After the spread of vegetarianism, Indian foods began to be classified into three main categories. Cooked vegetables, milk, fresh fruits, and honey were considered as 'satvika' foods. Foods that bring out the lowest and most base qualities of human behaviour were meat, liquor, garlic and spicy and sour foods, which were classified as 'tamasika'. Foods that give enough energy to carry out daily work are categorized as 'rajsika'.[32]

The Vedas not only give us a peek into what foods and spices were like back then, they also tell us a lot about the Vedic lifestyle and the rituals around food. For example, rice and ghee played an important role in the fire sacrifices. But one of the most remarkable statements that comes from this literature is the catchphrase that continues to echo even today. The words 'atithi devo bhava' originated from the *Taittiriya Upanishad*, embedded as three chapters of the *Yajur Veda*. It literally translates to 'the guest is God' and became part of the code of conduct for early Hindu society, becoming a tagline for the Indian tourism industry many centuries later. According to this concept, food or naivedya is an important part of a five-step worship programme, where every guest would enjoy a warm welcome, a lamp-lighting ritual, a rice-and-vermilion tilak and flower offerings.

Ayuh-sattva-balarogya-
sukha-priti-vivardhanah
rasyah snigdhah sthira hrdya
aharah sattvika-priyah
katv-amla-lavanaty-usna-
tiksna-ruksa-vidahinah
ahara rajasasyesta
duhkha-sokamaya-pradah
yata-yamam gata-rasam
puti paryusitam ca yat
ucchistam api camedhyam
bhojanam tamasa-priyam

Foods in the mode of goodness increase the duration of life, purify one's existence and give strength, health, happiness and satisfaction. Such nourishing foods are sweet, juicy, fattening and palatable. Foods that are too bitter, too sour, salty, pungent, dry and hot, are liked by people in the modes of passion. Such foods cause pain, distress, and disease. Food cooked more than three hours before being eaten, which is tasteless, stale, putrid, decomposed and unclean, is food liked by people in the mode of ignorance.

This is an excerpt from the Bhagavad Gita, chapter 17. Besides the Vedas, three other popular Hindu texts, the Bhagavad Gita, the Ramayana and the Mahabharata, contain references to food. While the Vedas gave us much information on the kinds of foods that were eaten during the Vedic times, the other three works teach us how to behave with a fellow diner, the importance of spiritual offerings, the sharing of food, and other dietary rules—all with the intention of developing one's spiritual character. Culinary ingredients and dishes are mentioned sparingly, though, restricted to a variety of fruits, and to milk, curd, neem leaves, poha, saag, berries, peanuts, porridge and laddoos.

I find the concept of *Sita ki Rasoi* the most fascinating among all the scriptural references. Even today, there exists a small space in Ayodhya that is believed to be Sita's kitchen, where worshippers can catch a glimpse of a symbolic rolling pin and board.[33] While Sita and Draupadi were both regarded as good cooks and hosts, there is mention of a male chef too in the scriptures. King Nala was known to have impeccable culinary skills and his superpower included his ability to cook without fire. He also wrote a cookbook called *Paka Darpanam,* which delves into the qualities of a good food server and features recipes such as the earlier-mentioned odana, supa (preparation of legumes), sarpis or ghee, mamsa (preparation of meat), saka (preparation of vegetables) and bhaksya (munchies). Besides, there is mention of rice pudding, a type of khichdi, milk, buttermilk, curd rice, biryani and drinks.[34] Bheema is credited as being as a good cook, but he would cook only for himself. Both the male cooks are referred to in the Mahabharata.

Patram puṣpam phalam toyam
yo me bhaktyā prayacchati
tad aham bhakty-upahṛtam
aśnāmi prayatātmanaḥ

If one offers Me with love and devotion a leaf, a flower, fruit and water,
I will accept it.
——Bhagavad Gita (9.26)

Some of the most unique food traditions to come out of Hinduism can be found in the temple cuisines of India; though in some parts of the world, like China, Vietnam, Korea and Japan, a Buddhist version of temple cuisine is practised. In the Indian subcontinent, temple cuisine flourished—from the banks of the Ganges in Rishikesh and Varanasi, to Madurai and Kanyakumari in the southernmost end. It spread across the west and the heart of the country, giving us recipes that are peculiar to the deity they are being offered in the name of.

One commonality among temple foods, be it at the Venkateswara temple in Andhra Pradesh, the Jagannath temple in Odisha, the Golden Temple in Punjab or the Nathdwara mandir in Rajasthan, is that the chefs (mostly male) cook food without tasting it before it is served to the deity. I have heard of Buddhist monks in Japan blessing meals in a ceremonial ritual before diners eat at Michelin-starred Buddhist restaurants. Similarly, Indian temple food or prasadam is always blessed and chanted upon.

Originally, temple food was also locavore and only made use of produce that grew in the neighbouring farmlands. The deity was offered the first harvest, and the chefs, who, by the way, practised an intense kitchen hierarchy, cooked following the rules of ancient Indian culinary wisdom, such as not mixing acidic food with milky food, or simple guidelines such as eating seasonal, avoiding tamasika ingredients, and so on. Small portions of food offered to the deity were then mixed with larger portions cooked for the masses, and rows of devotees were served the food for free. This continues even today and sometimes the speciality sweets were charged for.

Prasadam is mainly devoid of egg, meat, fish, onion and garlic. And while it is predominantly a combination of dal, rice, sometimes chapati/flatbread, pickle, papad and a sweet offering, depending on where you are in the country, certain dishes will vary. In the temples of south India today, you will find idli, upma, indigenous varieties of rice like matta, navara and unakkalari (rice with bran), while in north India you'll find wheat, chunks of soya, paneer, white butter and other dairy-based products. The underdog vegetables that don't make it to urban homes, like yams, roots, tubers, pumpkin and gourds, find common place in temple cuisines across the country.

Besides the Hindu scriptures, Jain and Buddhist texts also throw light on the food of ancient India. The post-Vedic society was mainly divided according to the lines of hierarchy between the Brahmins, Kshatriyas, Vaishyas, and Shudras, and each varna had its own cultural and culinary habits. With the advent of Jainism and Buddhism, newer nuances and layers were added to the religious fabric of the subcontinent, and ideas about what was kosher and what wasn't also changed drastically. Both religions form an integral part of the cultural base that evolved on the Indian subcontinent.

For me, the earliest memory of a Jain meal is from school. In the Introduction, I have told you about my best friend, whose tiffin I have eaten more than my own. Although her family cooked bearing in mind a lot of culinary restrictions, she ate all things magnificently cooked, adhering to the principles of Jainism. There is one thing I learnt from her dabba while eating a plate of 'batata' poha: Jains use dense raw banana in almost every dish where potato is crucial, including 'aloo' paratha.

Jainism is a prehistoric religion that started with the birth of Rishabhdev, and religious experts believe that this was even before the concept of time existed. Jainism talks of twenty-four tirthankaras (prophets), of whom Rishabhdev was the first and

Parshvanath the twenty-third tirthankara (872 BC–772 BC); the latter was followed by Mahavira (599 BC–527 BC).[35] Little is known about the food that Jains ate until Mahavira's time. The teachings of the twenty-three tirthankaras before Mahavira have been lost over time and hence, we do not find any sutras (aphorisms) even of Parshvanath's teachings today (there is no way to substantiate these claims).[36]

As a religion, Jainism predominantly developed in the plains of the middle and lower Ganges valley (present-day Bihar, eastern Uttar Pradesh, parts of Bengal and Jharkhand). Later, it expanded southwards and especially westwards (to Gujarat, Rajasthan, Delhi, Maharashtra and Karnataka).

I once met a Chinese-American chef who had just arrived to work in India. He complained to me that when he cooked abroad, all vegans had the same dietary rules, but in India, no vegetarian ate like another. To me, Jainism is the most palpable and foremost formulation of vegetarianism in the world, and it has distinctive features that separate it from Brahminical vegetarianism.

Jain dietary principles are based on the idea of jiva (living substance), ajiva (inanimate substance) and the concept of ahimsa (non-violence). Anything that has too much jiva is impermissible to eat and killing, or practising himsa (violence), is out of bounds for the Jain, which means animal meat and eggs are a no-no. Jains avoid underground or root vegetables and honey too, and it is interesting why that is so.

Their texts classify vanaspatikaya, or plants, into two categories—'sukshma', extremely microscopic, and 'badar', the category to which most plants belong. Badar is further divided into 'pratyek', having one body and one soul, like a leaf, and 'sadharan', having infinite souls in one body. As root vegetables are considered to have infinite souls, they were forbidden for consumption. The underlying idea is to determine how many jivas are present in each food before it can be considered as acceptable to eat.[37]

Unlike what is popularly believed, vegetables like the potato, carrot and radish are not mentioned in the ancient Jain scriptures as they came to India much later. Many roots, tubers and vegetables mentioned in the Agamas (religious texts), like hirela, sirela, sheer vidari, feluti, podvel and sheval, may have become extinct over time. The recognizable foods that find mention in ancient Jain texts include ginger, garlic, honey, figs, sugarcane, neem, milk, curd, jaggery, oil and ghee, confirming that they were indigenously Indian.[38]

For Jains, vegetarianism intensifies as one moves from one season to the next. There are different rules for monsoon and for summer, for instance. And, as one advances in the spiritual path, other foods and ingredients, such as salt, ice and rice, are avoided.

In the Jain scriptures food is mentioned sparingly and isn't emphasized as much as it has been in the Vedas. However, the Jain scriptures do talk about the presence of 84 lakh main living species in the world, 14 lakh of them being from the plant kingdom. *Agama* literature further divides plants along several botanical criteria, such as plants with seeds in their roots, in their trunks, in their fruit, and so on. Gods and goddesses too are said to reincarnate in the form of plants.[39]

Then, between the sixth and fourth centuries BC, in a part of the Indian subcontinent around Nepal, another religion was born, founded by Gautama Buddha.[40] There are a lot of similarities between Jainism and Buddhism. Not only are the life stories of their founders or prophets almost identical, both religions have created a community of monks and nuns, both believe in reincarnation and the concept of the soul, share similar ethical values and pursue the final goal of nirvana or moksha, which ends the cycle of rebirth.

Unlike Jainism, Buddhism doesn't prescribe severe food restrictions, but it does have its own rules. As a food reporter, I think the biggest and most far-reaching manifestation of the Buddhist way of eating can be found in the current times. From the insane popularity of 'Buddha bowls', which are designed around the religion's most basic principle, to accepting what is put into your bowl, to the refined shojin ryori cuisine, and the Zen Buddhist way of eating I mentioned in the Introduction, Buddhist culinary ways have been trending.

My research indicates that the thumb rule for monks ever since the Buddha's time was to accept food in the form of alms. This meant that eating meat was permissible, as one could not reject what was put into their bowl. Buddhist scriptures drop cues about food sparingly, so it is difficult to gauge what foods were available in the Buddha's time. The Tamil Buddhist scripture *Manimekalai*, written by the Tamil poet Sattanar (eleven verses of the Sangam literature have been attributed to him), dates to around the sixth century BC. The author is identified as a Buddhist grain merchant, and the book has references to the cow, its milk and ghee, and beef.[41]

There has always been a lot of controversy around what the Buddha ate, especially in respect of his last meal. But we will come to that later. Research brings out that as Prince Gautama, he ate high-quality meals in the palace—partaking of dishes like sali, a variety of long-grained rice, barley cakes, ghee, curd, butter, a variety of meats like beef, goat, fowl, venison and freshwater fish, fruits, vegetables, dry grains and even liquor.[42]

Once on his path to enlightenment, the Buddha's meals moved to jujube fruit, sesame seed and 'one grain of rice'. He also consumed honey and curd. The *Vinaya Pitaka* (monastic code) contains a large number of rules pertaining to Buddhist food. The Buddha spoke in favour of yagu, a gruel of rice, water and salt, to be eaten in the morning. Yagu was also made out of sour milk, curd, fruit and edible leaves. Once again, there is mention of the odana, boiled rice mixed with ghee, fruit or meat, sattu, baked wheat, barley, millet or gram flour, rolled into a ball or formed into a paste, kummasa (a boiled mixture of barley or pulses), maccho or fish and mamsa or meat. Leafy greens, vegetables, lotus stem, gourds, cucumber and aubergine were permitted to be consumed. Garlic and a certain kind of onion or leek was forbidden.

There is mention of panasa (jackfruit), breadfruit, tala (palmyra fruit), coconut, mango, jamun (rose apple) and banana. Sadavana, a fruit pudding, is also mentioned. Juices were made from mango, rose apple, banana, honeyfruit, water lily stem, grapes and sugarcane.[43]

Buddhists were permitted to season food with salt, pepper, cumin, turmeric, ginger, mustard, clove and haritaki or myrobalan, an ancient ingredient that is one of the three ingredients of triphala, arguably one of Ayurveda's most commonly used formulations. The medicinal ingredients in food include sappi (ghee), navanita (fresh butter), tela (sesame, mustard or castor oil), madhu or honey, phanita and sugarcane molasses.

The Buddha's last meal still remains shrouded in mystery. Some researchers say that it was a combination of bamboo shoot and a broth made from the five 'elements' of the cow, namely milk, curd, butter, urine and dung. It is also thought to have included a certain ingredient called 'sukara-maddava', which scholars describe as a mushroom that pigs love (maybe a certain kind of truffle) or tender pork itself.[44]

The Buddha did not make vegetarianism compulsory, as long as one was sure the animal had not been specially killed for their consumption. In Buddhism, a few things are forbidden, such as alcohol and wild meat (of elephant, horse, dog, snake, lion, tiger, leopard, bear and hyena).

The *Jataka Tales*, which are stories from the Buddha's life, are an interesting source of food references pertaining to Buddhism. The tales belong to the Theravada branch of Buddhism and were written around the fourth century BC.[45] It's interesting that some of these stories predate the Buddha's birth, as these are also stories about his incarnations in animal form before he was born in human form.

In these tales I stumbled upon several references to rice eaten in various forms—dried, in a porridge, or eaten as steamed dumplings. Besides, ingredients like honey out of the honeycomb, pork, chaff (husks of corn), edible roots of a flowering plants, turnip, jamun, a fruit known as seppani, tender shoots, lotus stalk, crab, palmyra fruit and myrobalan also find mention. There are also references to dishes like a certain kind of curry and gruel, which tell us that the mushy porridge continued to please the palate of the Indian subcontinent for years.

Therigatha, a set of Buddhist scriptures, details food categories such as 'sakunabhattam', food for the birds; 'sadukama', sweet foods; 'ratthapindam', food served as alms; 'pandam', food for alms or lumps of food; 'parabhattam', food for others; and 'annapanassa', meaning food and drinks. It seems that most of the cooking during this period was done in earthenware pots, and bowls played an important role in a Buddhist monk's life.

Besides these more popular religions, the Indian subcontinent was also home to a variety of religions in the centuries that followed. But Hinduism, Jainism and Buddhism were the three oldest religions that gave shape to the various forms of modern Indian dishes—like the apupa leading to the malpua of today, or the odana leading to perhaps some form of khichdi. The dos and don'ts mentioned in the texts of these religions, the scriptures pertaining to the caste system in Hinduism, the Jain monastic code and the rules of Ayurveda further tightened the universe of food for Indians in terms of what they could and could not eat. In fact, religion continues to determine the way the subcontinent eats, for example, through a nationwide beef ban or through what is served as the modern prasadam (the International Society for Krishna Consciousness is known for serving everything from a whole wheat cake to kulfi to devotees). Thus, these three religions did set the tone for what was to come for centuries.

3

INDIAN ROYALTY

I've eaten my way through Gujarat. The land of khandvi and undhiyu threw at me dishes I never associated with Gujarati cuisine. Take a chickpea flour goop called locho, for example, a speciality from Surat that looks exactly like scrambled eggs; or the embarrassingly delicious pizza topped with ketchup and cheese, which you will find at a zillion food trucks in Ahmedabad; or a Maharashtrian dish called usal, which I found in Vadodara (earlier Baroda). The streets here are strewn with shops selling the lentils-and-bean mix usually eaten with bread, and it made me wonder how this Maharashtrian dish became such a hot (literally too) item in the town of Vadodara.

Interestingly, Maharashtrian food has a deep influence on this region. To begin at the beginning, the Maratha kingdom formally came into being in the second half of the seventeenth century, mainly around 1674, when Shivaji founded a new Hindu kingdom in the Deccan. All through the fourteenth, fifteenth and sixteenth centuries, the Sultans more or less ruled this heart of India, and its cuisine too was influenced by their way of eating. But for centuries, religious and social movements had been brewing there. So, while smaller non-Muslim kingdoms always existed, it was Muslim rule that reigned supreme. With Shivaji came a reformation, and the Maratha state was founded.

At its peak, the Maratha kingdom stretched from Tamil Nadu in the south of India to Khyber in the north and to West Bengal in the east, and so this kingdom obviously adopted flavours from all of its adjoining states. For centuries the Marathas and Mughals fought constant battles, in the process also influencing each other as well as their respective cuisines. But a major shift happened only when the fourth of the Peshwas (prime minister) in Maharashtra, Madhavrao I, decided to give semi-autonomy to leaders from far-flung kingdoms, like the Holkars of Indore and Malwa, the Scindias of Gwalior and Ujjain, and the Gaekwads of Baroda.[1] These exchanges led to extensive cross-pollination of ideas and cultures, and a period when the cauldron of royal Marathi cuisine finally began to stir with new influences. That was probably when a dish of strong Maharashtrian influence infiltrated into a Gujarati town.

This was especially true when one of the wealthiest princely families of India, the Gaekwads, who were originally from Pune, set up their base in Baroda. Their kitchen and culture saw influences pouring in from the Mughals, the Marathas, and from the Gwalior, Tanjore and Kolhapuri 'gharanas', leading to a cuisine that was as diverse as the spice box you'll find in the average Indian kitchen.

And this is just one example of how royalty influenced food in India. The connection between food and royalty in India is at least 2,000 years old. Back then too, kingdoms like Magadha and Nanda existed on the Indian subcontinent, but it was around 321 BC, after King Alexander's death, that the first major kingdom, the Mauryan Empire, was formed. In my imagination, the visions of this period seem to be a bit of a combination of Amish Tripathi's books and the sets of *Bahubali*, complete with massive pillars, dancing peacocks, and bejewelled elephants—only, it is neither. (Random trivia: *Bahubali* was inspired by the Kalachuri dynasty, whose power declined with the Chalukyas.)

The Mauryan dynasty was founded by Chandragupta Maurya. It was located at the confluence of the Ganga and Gandak rivers, and its capital Pataliputra is present-day Patna. Not much literature can be found on what the Mauryans ate, but from their Aramaic style of writing, road construction patterns and choice of art and architecture, one can assume that the empire was highly influenced by the Persian kingdom, and we can assume that so must have been its food.[2]

During this phase, wheat and barley were still the predominant crops on the subcontinent. In the previous chapters, we have already established the commonalities between the Persian and Indian societies, and the Mauryan kingdom was a fitting illustration of this. Soma, ghee, curd, milk and honey find mention and ample usage in both societies.

An interesting source from which we can learn more about the Mauryan way of life is Megasthenes's *Indica*. The author was a Greek traveller, an ambassador at the time of a Mauryan king. Megasthenes jotted down observations about the Indian people in his book. In a chapter titled 'Of the suppers of the Indians', we get vague indications of how Indians ate their supper: Tripod-like tables were placed before each person, and they ate out of a golden bowl placed on it. In the bowl, first rice is put, 'boiled like how one would boil barley', then many additions were served. It is unclear what these additions were though.[3]

Meat was mainly eaten after a sacrifice, and included animals such as bull, deer, antelope, buffalo, sheep, pig, chicken, peacock, hare, hedgehog, porcupine and tortoise. The society was ritualistic, and different gods were pleased using different sacrificial meats—barren cows were used to appease Agni, bulls for Indra, the ox for Vishnu and so on. The masses were mainly vegetarian, but the kings and their entourages ate meat. Non-vegetarian food was cooked for those who needed strength, like warriors or someone recuperating from an illness.

The *Arthashashtra*, one of the scriptures of this period, gives us a peek into the Mauryan kitchen. A handbook written by Kautilya (popularly known as Chanakya), a statesman and philosopher in Chandragupta Maurya's court, the *Arthashashtra* speaks about the rules of everything, from running an empire to conducting one's life. Here you'll find mention of certain 'intoxicating drinks' made of fresh juice, honey, curd and grain (mainly rice or barley). One of these could easily be an early version of beer, and Megasthenes confirms this in *Indica*.[4]

So far back in history, even for the royals, food didn't include any extravagance. It was need-based. The king was responsible for food security, with agricultural stocks kept in the royal granaries, and he directed the retention of annual produce, especially for the relief of the poor. Salt was of tremendous value. The *Arthashashtra* says, 'The superintendent of ocean-mines (khanyadhyakshah) shall attend to the collection of conch-shells, diamonds, precious stones, pearls, corals and salt (kshara) and also regulate the commerce in the above commodities.'[5]

Once the salt was crystallized, the superintendent of salt collected the share of the salt that was due to the government. Stringent rules were laid down for its distribution. For example, if it was imported from another region, the king was to be paid given one-sixth of the amount, and its adulteration was punishable with the highest degree of comeuppance.[6]

Furthermore, the *Arthashashtra* confirms the existence of a complex commercial model. Agricultural produce was known as 'sita'. The kingdom levied taxes, allowed the bartering and borrowing of grain, manufactured oils and grew rice. Sugar was manufactured from sugarcane juice and there is a mention of 'phanita', a decoction of jaggery, sugar candy and granulated sugar. Sweeteners were extracted from beehives (honey). The juice of grapes was also called 'madhu',[7] and this is another indication that grapes could be found in India before the Central Asian traders brought them in.

The serial juicer in me finds this superfood smoothie-like blend, which the book mentions, the most exotic: a mixture of the juices of sugarcane, grapes, jaggery, honey, jamun extract, jaka tree essence, long pepper, essence of chirbhita (a variety of gourd), cucumber, mango and two medicinal plants, myrobalan and meshasringa. This mixture could be stored for months together and was consumed for medical benefits, though we don't know exactly how it impacted the body.[8]

The chapters mention a variety of legumes and fruits, like karamarda, citron, jujube, badara, and other acidic fruits. There are references to condiments like pepper, ginger, cumin, white mustard, coriander and moringa; and to medicinal plants like kiratatikta (*Swertia chirayita*), choraka (angelica root) and maruvaka (marjoram), which still find modern-day use in the treatment of ailments like diabetes, congestion and infections.[9]

For me, the *Arthashashtra* was a treasure trove when it came to referencing food ingredients of the Mauryan time. There is mention of dried fish, and grains are described using the forms in which they were eaten, like pounded (kshunna), frayed (ghrishta), reduced to flour (pishta), fried (bhrashta), or dried after being soaked in water and turned into gruel. They also extracted oils out of linseed (atasi), neem leaves (nimba), wood apple (kapittha), sesame seeds (kusumba), mahua (madhúka), the Indian almond tree (ingudi), cottonseed, flaxseed and also a type of kidney bean, which means that these are indigenous Indian trees and crops. Apart from talking about ingredients and cooking methods, the book also delves into weights and measurements, and storage and distribution of grains.[10] A similarity that I found between the Jain Agamas and the *Arthasashtra* is the mention of a variety of bulbous roots or kandamula. The connection fits, because Chandragupta Maurya had, after all, abdicated his throne for his son Bindusara and become a Jain monk.

Bindusara's son Ashoka became a patron of Buddhism, and that impacted Indian cuisine once again. Here is what one of Ashoka's pillar edicts says:

. . . various animals were declared to be protected—parrots, mainas, aruna, ruddy geese, wild ducks, nandimukhas, gelatas, bats, queen ants, terrapins, boneless fish, vedareyaka, gangapuputaka, sankiya fish, tortoises, porcupines, squirrels, deer, bulls, okapinda, wild asses, wild pigeons, domestic pigeons and all four-footed creatures that are neither useful nor edible. Those nanny goats, ewes and sows which are with young or giving milk to their young are protected, and so are young ones less than six months old. Cocks are not to be caponized, husks hiding living beings are not to be burnt and forests are not to be burnt either without reason or to kill creatures. One animal is not to be fed to another. On the three Caturmasis, the three days of Tisa and during the fourteenth and fifteenth of the Uposatha, fish are protected and not to be sold. During these days animals are not to be killed in the elephant reserves or the fish reserves either. On the eighth of every fortnight, on the fourteenth and fifteenth, on Tisa, Punarvasu, the three Caturmasis and other auspicious days, bulls are not to be castrated, billy goats, rams, boars and other animals that are usually castrated are not to be. On Tisa, Punarvasu, Caturmasis and the fortnight of Caturmasis, horses and bullocks are not to be branded.

Ashoka, who ruled an estimated population of 30 million, much larger than that of any of the contemporary Hellenistic kingdoms, banned animal killing.[11] His famous rock edicts talk about everything from religious tolerance and generosity towards priests to the planting of fruit and shade trees. So much so that even fishing was forbidden, and husk sheaves, which were ordinarily set on fire, could not be burnt, as many living things in them would be killed. The Mauryan economy was anyway an agricultural one, but with Ashoka's rules, many Indians became vegetarian. Killing of animals was forbidden and there emerged a remarkable vegetarian movement on the subcontinent.

Towards the south of India, the Pallava dynasty was contributing to India's culinary legacy. The Pallavas originated as pastoralists on the Deccan plateau, and by the fourth century BC they had established Kanci, modern-day Kanchipuram, as their capital.[12] By then this part of the Indian subcontinent had seen a substantial economic boom. The Pallavas expanded their influence eastwards, with their merchants using the centuries-old trade routes that linked India and China to Rome via South-East Asia, the Arabian Peninsula and East

Africa. This means that there was ample cultural exchange between South-East Asian nations and south India, perhaps a starting point for us to understand why today there are so many cultural similarities between these two regions.

There is some research that points to how many South-East Asian customs and culinary trends may have been derived from the Pallava and Chola dynasties' expansion eastwards. Take, for instance, the existence of curries in both our kitchens. Though curry is common in many other Asian countries, like Japan, Vietnam, Korea and Cambodia, Thai and Malay curries share common ingredients with ours. Their use of spices such as turmeric, coconut or coconut milk, and the technique of sautéing curry pastes, followed by diluting it with a liquid, are all very similar to the Indian way. We will also talk about the word 'curry' itself, which came about much later, a term that repels Indian food writers and cookbook authors, surprisingly abroad more than in India, in the Conclusion.

The Pallava dynasty made way for the Cholas. This was an empire known for its fabulous feasts. The kingdom formed one of the three great royal divisions of early southern India—with the other two being those of the Pandiyas further southwards and of the Cheras in the west. The Chola kingdom was in existence even during 300 BC–250 BC, as mentioned in the inscriptions of King Ashoka, where it is called the 'Choda' dynasty. There he was referring to the early Cholas.

I'm talking of the period of the medieval Cholas, for whom food was beyond sustenance. At their peak, the south Indian kingdom had grown wealthy and had dominance over sea trade. It had conquered Sri Lanka, the Andaman and Nicobar Islands and some parts of South-East Asia as well—the islands of Sumatra, Java and Bali, and the southern part of the Malay peninsula.

The Cholas were probably one of the earliest Asian empires to have experimented in overseas trade and expansion, and with the help of their famous Chola navy had mastered the art of seafaring, which aided further expansion and adventures outside the Indian subcontinent. Obviously, they prompted a lot of culture and culinary exchange, especially with the Chinese and Arabs, with whom they exchanged silk and spices. Since the Cholas had access to luxurious Indian spices and the know-how to cook with these, local Indian cuisine benefited from and refined itself under their reign.

Literature from the Chola period talks about game meats such as boar and porcupine being consumed, a Chola prince gorging on wild fruits from the forest, like jamun, and vegetables like bamboo, elephant-foot yam and jackfruit.[13] The most interesting reference in their texts is to a snack from this period, which reminds me of bowls of sundal—roasted peanuts eaten with a sprinkling of fresh coconut and sold commonly on the streets—which I grab first thing on reaching Chennai. There is also mention of many varieties of millets, rice or wheat, and of sweets, like a toffee made out of jaggery, and spice-sprinkled fruit. One of the dishes mentioned in Chola poems consists of avarai beans (broad country beans) cooked in a tamarind gravy.[14] They also mentions angaya podi, a mixture of ginger, pepper and cumin seeds, which acted as an appetite stimulant and was had before or after the meal with a dash of sesame oil.[15] For me, the Chola kitchen is a slice of the most delicious piece of south Indian history.

There are also food references to be found in Sangam literature, which dates to centuries before the medieval Chola period and is one of the earliest documentations of ancient Tamil culture. Tamil literature is perhaps the only classical Indian literature in India which is non-Sanskrit. It is believed that Sangam literature spans three ages. The first Sangam was the gathering of the gods and sages and lasted for 4,400 years; the second was a collection of the works of 3,700 poets. Verses from both these Sangams appear to have been lost with the destruction of the civilizations. The third one lasted for 1,850 years, resulting in an output of 449 poems, and is among the earliest available Tamil literature.

The three main kingdoms that flourished in the Sangam period were the Cheras, the Cholas, and the Pandyas. And several poets rose from among the common folk to speak about everyday affairs, life concerns, and the culture and habits of the commoners. In their poems you'll find food references too explaining the early food habits of Tamil society.

Rice played an important role in the cuisine, and took many forms in these poems. I found mention of plain steamed rice, rice eaten with curry, rice turned into balls, rice cooked in milk with honey and white rice eaten with a thick curry made of crab flesh. They also ate a variety of millets, smoked and mashed aubergine, tangy frothy buttermilk, pork cooked in ghee, and drank fermented liquor and toddy.[16]

The Cholas for the most part ate really well, with access to produce like spinach, tubers, ridge gourd, pulses, cereals, legumes, honey, raw mango, ghee and lentils. Puffed rice and pickles were made too. They cooked on a live fire, and fried, sun-dried and pickled their ingredients. They also consumed a variety of unusual meats, like that of tortoise, porcupine, monitor lizard and sometimes even rat. I did say they ate well in 'most parts'.

The Sangam era markets must have been interesting places that gave a glimpse into Tamil society of the time. There is no mention of money in these texts, but it seems like exchange happened via barter. A poet in *Purananuru* (a Tamil poetic work) says, 'They sell fish and bring in the boats heaps of paddy which fill the house.' Poet Kannanar says, 'Those selling honey and edible roots exchange them for fish oil and wine. They barter sugarcane and roasted rice for toddy and venison.'[17]

As in Vedic society, the theme of hospitality is common here too. Though hunger is also a recurring theme in the works of the poets, they emphasize that a guest should never be allowed to leave a home without at least tasting something.

More food references pour in through *Ten Idylls*, an anthology of ten poems known as *Pattuppattu*, a part of Sangam literature. It mentions varieties of rice, bamboo and tinai rice (foxtail millet) as staples that were either boiled or roasted. There is mention of beans, roots, valli (a kind of sweet potato), jackfruit, plantain, tender coconut, areca nut, pepper, saffron, turmeric, ginger, sempu (a type of dense vegetable) and honey. The poems confirm the presence of rice toddy. There was ample dairy in the form of curd, ghee and milk. Two kinds of meat variations have been mentioned—fresh meat and dried meat. Ram, pig, cow, deer, fowl, iguana, fish and crab were relished.[18]

Besides narrating what Tamilians ate, the texts go deeper to explain the topography of the land through different landscapes called thinais. 'Kurinchi' were hilly or mountainous terrains, full of verdant slopes, home to hunters and nomads. 'Mullai' were the forests and grasslands meant for cattle herders. 'Palai' were lands with minimum vegetation or deserts; 'neithal' consisted of the vast coastline; and 'murudham' were the fertile farmlands.[19]

Gruel finds mention again here. This deep into my research, I can now confirm that our ancestors across the subcontinent were obsessed with porridge. There is mention of a dish called kanjika made of rice. Perhaps this was the predecessor of the current-day rice kanji or south Asian congee (the word derives from the Tamil word kanji). The Chola porridge had medicinal value and was essentially a fermented rice soup flavoured with long pepper and ginger.

This could be during the Chola or the Pandya period, but Sangam literature does mention ingredients such as cardamom, pepper, mustard, cumin and khus khus. Lime and salt were taxable commodities. There is also mention of other foods and ingredients such as toddy, fish oil, tamarind, barley, wheat, sorghum, and millet.

Sangam literature mentions women labouring in the fields, and has descriptions of diverse farming practices, like levelling, transplanting of the paddy, hoeing, weeding, threshing, winnowing, and so on. *Civaka Cintamani*, one of the Tamil epics from Sangam literature, describes the happiness of the peasant community of this age. The main crops during this period were sugarcane, pulses like lab lab (hyacinth) and cajunas or pigeon peas.[20]

Tamil poems in the *Manimekalai* date to much after the Chola period (approximately AD 890 to AD 950). They too give us a peek into this region's food habits centuries later. The verses set in Kaveripattinam (now Poompuhar, Tamil Nadu) and in Nainatheevu (now Jaffna in Sri Lanka) are about a Cholan prince, Udayakumaran. References to mango, areca nut or supari, bananas, sugarcane, jamun, milk, bitter orange, saffron, lime, bamboo, screwpine, gamboge (a tropical tree bearing yellow fruits), coconut, wood apple, jujube, rice paddy, salt, sheep meat, rice pudding and certain sweet spices are mentioned in these texts.[21]

Rice has always played an important role in the region. It was a staple in south India, and since it grew in abundance, it was bartered and accepted as a common measure of value. The texts mention various ways in which rice was eaten—in the form of cakes and soups, fresh and fermented, and, of course, as gruel again.

Centuries after the Chola empire, a south Indian royal kitchen that became prominent was from the Vijayanagar empire, dating from AD 1336 to AD 1565. The empire was founded by the brothers Harihara and Bukka with the blessings of a sage called Vidyaranya.[22] Vijayanagar established its core in Anegondhi, on the banks of the Tungabhadra river (55 km away from present-day Bellary in Karnataka), and gradually spread over the entire Deccan. Though the empire existed over many centuries, it was only during the reign of the Telugu-speaking king Krishnadevaraya (post AD 1509) that the golden age of Vijayanagar began. I tried to trace the evolution of Indian cuisine from this royal kitchen.

Vijayanagar partook in enormous trade and commerce with the outside world. By the time of Krishnadevraya's regime, the Europeans had begun to establish contacts along the west coast of India, and this opened the market for the spices of the western ghats. The Europeans were looking to establish markets for spices outside of the Arab world, and Indian merchants realized that the new buyers provided them better opportunities than the Arabs did. South India was rich with natural resources like sandalwood, spices (and diamonds) and the governing class did everything to promote their cash crops. Take, for instance, a rule established by the Vijayanagar monarchs to offer irrigated land free of tax for a specified period of time to cultivators so that the nomadic farmers could settle down in this region.[23]

Predictably, rice was a staple and an important grain, especially for the upper classes and, ironically (from today's perspective), the lower castes were mocked for consuming too much millet. It is the reverse now, with millets becoming an urban obsession. Rice featured in prominent rituals and had great social value. This is reinforced again in the *Sanatkumara Charite*, an important piece of Kannada literature from the medieval period (AD 1485) that mentions the consumption of at least twelve varieties of rice at royal weddings. It was considered the food of the gods and was never missing from feasts; millets, on the other hand, seldom made an appearance at feasts.[24] Vijayanagar grew rice in paddies; they had a complex network of canals for water supply and drainage channels, and had sophisticated agricultural practices.

Texts from this period mention dishes such as chitranna, which is essentially lemon rice, pakvanna or cooked rice, and mosaru butti or curd rice.[25] The average local ate sorghum, ragi and bajra. A typical meal during this period was similar to what people from south India eat today—it starts with a helping of salt and pickles made of mango, lemon, ginger, Indian gooseberry, and probably even a helping of raw mango, followed by rice and other items.

The Vijayanagar traders dealt not only in spices like ginger, pepper and cardamom, but also in honey, wax, gum, resin, dyes, scented woods and medicinal plants like myrobalan.

A good insight into the history of edibles of this empire can be had from the words of Ibn Battuta, who famously visited Vijayanagar around AD 1336– AD 1357. He describes the meal he ate with the Muslim chief of Honavar as a one full of pickled peppers, ginger, lemon and mangoes, happala or papadum and sandige or vadams.[26] If you think about it, you are likely to eat a meal like this in many regions of Karnataka even today.

In *Bhujabali Charitre,* another work of Karnataka literature compiled around AD 1614, the poet Panchabana talks about something called tilada, or cooked vegetables seasoned with something that is identical to what we use in a tadka even today—a splattering of cumin seeds, lentil, fenugreek, mustard, black sesame and pepper, all cooked in clarified butter. One recipe has a paste of black gram turned into idli, vada and dosa.

The people of the Vijayanagar kingdom ate fruits like figs and plantains. Some researchers also believed they ate apples. Although commercial production of apples was started only in the 1800s by the British in the Kulu Valley, sufi Amir Khusro mentioned apples in India in about AD 1300 and we know that the Mughals grew them abundantly too. Other produce that was used amply in cooking included aubergine, pumpkin, gourds, jackfruit, drumsticks and magge or cucumber. It is interesting to note that so far in my research, cucumbers never showed up in the way they did for this period, in this region. Incidentally, according to the National Horticulture Board, confirms Karnataka is the second largest grower of cucumbers in India. Cucumbers did, in fact, originate in India and have been a part of the subcontinent for over 4,000 years now.

The most interesting among the poetic renditions of Vijayanagar is the work of Kanakadasa (AD 1509– AD 1609). The poet's commentary on the lifestyle of Vijayanagar reminded me of the buzzing streets of Seville. As you'd find tiny tapas bars selling small bites and vino there, in Vijayanagar too there were toddy shops that served a range of salted snacks to be eaten along with the liquor, says Kanakadasa. Describing the mood on the streets, he talks about how people 'drank and babbled'. The colourful marketplaces sold coconut, jackfruit, orange, mango, sweet citrus, guava, grapes, pomegranate, wood apple, inknut, berries, mangosteen, and some wild berries and grasses, such as Cyperus pertenuis. The 'bhuktashalas' or establishments also served panaka (cold jaggery water) and kenemosaranna (curd rice), and since orthodox Brahmins could not eat food cooked by people of other castes, so secluded quarters called 'ekantanilaya' were built for them.[27]

Lakshmisa, a Kannadiga Brahmin whose most important work includes the *Jaimini Bharata* (a version of the Mahabharata), provides us with very delicate details about the Vijayanagara kingdom. He talks about fruits being eaten in a pulverized form, and this could maybe point towards India's ancient juicer. The Telugu poet Srinatha, who lived in the first half of the fifteenth century, describes the food of the people of Palnad district in the Andhra part of the Vijayanagar empire as 'millet porridge, fermented millet, cooked millet and millet stuff. Except for millet they have nothing to eat and the cooked rice of the sanna variety is unknown to them'. Sarvajna, another Kannada poet and philosopher of the sixteenth century, confirms the abundance of millets in this region, while Purandara Dasa, a saint from around the same period, mentions kesakki, a dish made of a cheap variety of red rice; guggari, a dish of boiled or half-boiled peas or pulses and grits of grain; and godduli or plain soup.[28]

Vijayanagar also cooked a variety of sweetmeats, such as payasa or rice porridge; kadubu or crescent-shaped rice dumplings, which are eaten in Karnataka even today; vermicelli or sevige; sikarane or fruit salad; and laddige or laddoos. These sweets were mainly for the royals and nobles, and not for the average man; the commoners mostly ate a combination of pulses, vegetables and millets.

Apart from food ingredients and preparations, food presentation also finds mention in the works of some poets. Hospitality has always reigned supreme on the Indian subcontinent; and the following lines from Ibn Battuta, the Moroccan scholar and explorer, emphasize just that. In *Rihla*, a written account of his journey to India, he says,

She holds a large copper ladle with which she picks up a ladleful of rice and serves it on to the dish, pours ghee over it and adds pickles . . . when the food placed by her on the dish is consumed, she takes up a second spoonful of rice and serves a cooked fowl on a plate, and rice is eaten with that also. When the second course is over she takes another ladleful and serves another variety of chicken, which is also eaten with the rice. When the various kinds of chicken are consumed, fish of various kinds is served, with which one likewise eats rice. When all these courses are eaten, kushan (that is, curd-milk) is served which finishes the meal. When this is served, one knows that no further dishes are to follow. At the close, one drinks hot water; for cold water would harm the people in the rainy season.[29]

Besides Battuta, there is a line of European travellers like Nicoli dei Conti, Ludovico di Varthema and Duarte de Barbosa, who also came in touch with the southern shores. They had their first brush with mangoes, Indian spices, coconuts, cucumbers, the betel leaf, cotton, grapes, oranges, limes, pomegranates and jackfruits in India. An important dynasty that developed under the suzerainty of the Vijayanagar kingdom was that of the Wodeyars. When the Vijayanagar kingdom began to fade, it paved the way for Mughal power to grow north of the Tungabhadra river and for the rajas of Mysore to become powerful in the south. By the seventeenth century, the Wadiyars of Mysore, profiting from the conflict between the Mughals and the Marathas, had gained a stronghold in western India.

The Chalukyas were another important early medieval dynasty that left a mark on Indian cuisine. In *Manasollasa*, an early twentieth-century Sanskrit text composed by the Kalyani Chalukya (the Kannadiga dynasty is sometimes referred to as Kalyani Chalukya), King Someshvara III shares much socio-cultural information that gives us a view into the Chalukya dynasty's culinary life.

Manasollasa has several references to dishes that don't feel too unfamiliar, especially if you look at their descriptions. Take, for instance, manahvataka, a type of vada; a dish called gharika, which could be the predecessor of the Maharashtrian dish called gharge; katakatna, a preparation of pre-soaked peas; vatika, made of urad dal paste; purika or fried gram flour cakes; and parikas, which looked like modern-day bondas made of besan powder, salt, pepper, asafoetida and sugar.

There is also dhosaka, or dosai, and idarika or idli, both of which were then made only of pulses. A preparation called kavachandi particularly caught my attention. It consisted of plump pieces of mutton cooked with lentils or sprouts and spices, and fried with garlic, onions and vegetables such as brinjal and radish.[30] The dish may have tasted like a meat and vegetable curry, loaded with the freshest of spices that the Chalukyas had access to.

It is interesting how King Someshvara spoke of meats and their elaborate preparations: as if it is something right out of a Salvador Dali cookbook. If you have flipped through the legendary painter's food imaginations, you'll see how Someshvara talks just like that about carving liver in a globular shape, roasting it on a charcoal grill and frying it with spices, mixing it with curd and finishing it with mustard seeds.[31] There are mentions of roast tortoise meat, fish and fried crabs. One recipe even talks about mixing meats with a paste of lentils, spices, hyacinth beans, berries, onion, garlic and sour juice; this would be a rarity if you compare it with the south Indian dishes of today. As mentioned, the Chalukyas even ate rodent meat![32] But of a 'peculiar mice that lived in the fields near rivers'. Even today, a similar preparation of rat meat is consumed in the Mandya district of Karnataka.

Patrika, a traditional sweet, was named after the sheets of parchment that were used to write on since its layers were so fine. Back then, this medieval sweet was made of wheat flour, fried in ghee and dusted with ground sugar. There are mentions of veshta, a besan-based dish, and of vatika, a ball of ground urad paste too.

If I had to pick one royal kitchen whose menu piqued my tastebuds the most, after Vijayanagara's street-style toddy and curd-rice shops, it would have to be that of Tanjore. At the beginning of the chapter we discussed how the Marathas had a profound impact on the royal kitchens of the south, Tanjore being one of them. One of its offshoots was the development of the royal Thanjavur–Maratha cuisine. Tanjore had always been a breeding ground of culture, first because of the Cholas, and then the Nayaks, Telugu rulers from the sixteenth century. With the advent of the royal Marathas, starting from Vyankoji (Shivaji's half-brother) in 1676 to Shahaji in 1855, the Maratha rulers had an impact on the music, architecture, painting and, obviously, food of Tanjore (and some parts of Tamil Nadu). The cuisine still remained predominantly Tamil with some representation of Maharashtrian fare, evident from the Marathi names of the dishes. It was a coming together of a Kshatriya clan (the Marathas) and Brahmins (who had formed the Deshastha community in south India).[33]

Since this dynasty is comparatively more recent, for them access to ingredients was far better and the methods of cooking were more refined than earlier. Their meat dishes were fiery; like kesari maas, a saffron-laced mutton dish; mashyache kebab, which were fish fillets coated in poppy seed and chillies, pan-fried in ghee; komdiche kebab, which literally translates to chicken kebab; dhanedhar shunti, a delicate parcel of pounded lamb meat; and the komda pulao, rice made with chicken. The vegetarian dishes were nuanced too. There is khendatta, a variety of vegetable curry cooked with pulses; kelyachi bhaji, made of raw bananas; porathi kozhambu, a curry of brinjal with coconut and chillies; and shakar biranji, sweetened rice with almond, coconut and sultanas.

Of these, the story of sambhar's origin is the most popularly known and stands out the most. Sambhar is predominantly eaten in the southern parts of India, where you can find more than a hundred varieties of it. While a Tamilian dish called pitlai, made of tamarind, pepper and green gram dal, existed, no other dish matching sambhar's etymology can be traced in the literature of the region before this time.[34]

It is believed that sambhar came into being only when the Marathas began ruling in southern India, and was named after Sambhaji, Shivaji's eldest son. Apparently, Sambhaji was an ardent cook and was fond of a Marathi dish called aamti, which is a lentil-based stew soured with hints of kokum. The story goes that one day, the regular stash of kokum did not reach the Tanjore palace's kitchen on time. Instead of telling Sambhaji that aamti could not be made, the sous chef improvised by adding a dash of tamarind pulp, something the locals had been using for years for its tartness.[35] The dish became such a hit in the court kitchen that it was named sambhar after Sambhaji, and from Tanjore it spread to other parts of south India.

In the royal palaces of the Marathas, non-vegetarian and vegetarian cooking happened in separate areas. There was one space dedicated to making summer sherbets (sherbet khana), a room for cold water (aadhar khana), and something called the thatti mahal khana or halacha chool, for milk and tea. The palaces had a kottiyam, a typical south Indian home feature, where grain, groceries and oil were stored, and all departments had managers to oversee their functioning.[36]

Cleanliness and purity of the kitchen are common features of the Marathi and Tanjore kitchens. Food and cooking for the gods, naivedya, were sacred for the Thanjavur-Marathas, and the same philosophy extends to Tamilian-Brahmins too. The women were in charge of the kitchen, and utensils washed by the domestic help were washed again before use.[37] Thanjavur Marathas also had unique rituals, like circling the stove with a fistful of rice to be fed into the fire. Meals were cooked in brass pots, and ingredients like leftover rice and lentils were not carried over to another day. Sowla was the area where fresh meals were made, and it was not permissible to enter this space without bathing. Food was cooked on firewood, and on charcoal and gas in the later days.

The southern Indian and Maratha kingdoms, with the cultures of podis and polis, had several cross-influences emerging through the years. As I mentioned at the beginning of the chapter, the region of Baroda received culinary inputs from its linkage with the royal Maratha kingdom. But a Baroda-style pulao (smoked mutton and rice) also found its way into a recipe book put together by the Raste family that worked for the Peshwas, the ministers from Shrivardhan in Konkan. The Rastes got their name from the Persian word 'rast', which meant pure and fair. They occupied the prestigious

Raste Wada in Pune, and had palatial mansions and a buzzing kitchen that displayed supreme culinary finesse from this era.

The Rastes only used spring water to cook their meals; their kitchen was fitted with a copper-lined aqueduct that brought in water all the way from the Kondhwa and Wanowrie hills. They mainly cooked in copper or earthen vessels on coal or wood fire to give their fiery dishes—like Kolhapuri kombdiche sukke, Saoji mutton rassa and mundi rassa—a delightful smoky aroma. Like the larger Maratha palaces, their kitchen too had several rooms and separate areas for cooking, washing, sieving of grains and grinding of spices. There was an array of cooks (over twenty for a hundred members of the family) who dabbled with different cuisines. There were separate chefs for Gwalior-style dishes, Konkani dishes, Sangli-style food, and so on. Menus were planned in advance, with special treats lined up for Diwali, haldi-kumkum, and birthdays of family members. On these special days, the family ate out of silverware.[38]

Like most royals, the Marathas enjoyed hunting. This gave them access to game meats like wild boar, quail, venison and partridge. Lavang mirchi, a spicy variety of chilli, was used in abundance to flavour dishes, and dairy played an important role (not so much for the Maharashtrians in south India though), especially curd, which was used to thicken gravies. Everyday meals were no different from what can be found in the average Maharashtrian home even today—seafood or mutton-based gravy, vegetables, dal, varan, rice, bhakri or rice flour chapatis and thecha, an excessively hot and coarse spicy green chilli chutney.

Over the years, the Marathas set up their rule in various regions of India, including Jhansi, Indore, Vidarbha, Dhar, Dwas and Gwalior. So, their food too had influences pouring in from other states like Madhya Pradesh, Uttar Pradesh, Rajasthan and Karnataka. This resulted in dishes like bhutte ki kees, a delicacy of corn; keema samosa, which has a clear Madhya Pradesh connection; meat curries cooked in coconut, common among south Indian Marathas; rice flour rotis; and an array of chutneys made of peanut, coconut and poppy seed, and mutton pickle.

Many royal Maratha recipes were the results of the collective efforts of the Muslim and Hindu cooks who worked in the royal kitchens. The Maratha kitchens in the homes of common folk too changed when they came in touch with the British. Take, for instance, the last of the rulers of the Bhosle dynasty. He apparently had a European wing in the kitchen that whipped up jellies, stuffed meats, sauces, puffs and eggs in every possible variation.

A beautiful culinary legacy can be seen in the kitchens of the royal Scindia family. The Scindias were essentially chiefs of the Maratha empire under Shivaji (just like the Gaekwads and Holkars). Later, as the confederacy started breaking up due to political and aspirational reasons, they ruled as different families in different regions. Their menus continued to feature Maharashtrian dishes, ranging from varan-bhaat, jowar rotis, pasanda (a meat dish) to bhakar kombdi or chicken (especially the local kadaknath) cooked with dry coconut and spices, and included simple treats such as poha and bhakarwadis. Later, as

82

the family expanded its territories and as the Europeans began trading in India (as well as setting up their own armies), the Scindias hired French and English generals and commanders to revolutionize battle techniques and weapons to use against the British and Mughals. This also brought in European flavours to their cuisine and kitchens. Their cooks were trained to make soufflés, pasta, pastries and pies. From having a traditional kitchen they went on to use built-in rotisseries, Dutch ovens, stoves, grills and underground deep-freezers, which are still on display in their royal museum.

It was the Scindias who helped put the Mughal emperor Alam Shah back on the throne in Delhi and pushed out the Afghans (Ahmed Shah Durrani) who were reigning then. The Scindias's proximity to the Mughal court, and their hiring of khansamas also brought changes to their kitchens and influences from the north Indian and Mughlai cooking styles. This added Muslim-style salans, biryanis and pulaos to their menus, which weren't common features earlier. One Indian dish to come out of this period (late eighteenth century) is the famous bhatti pulao, a mutton pulao stuffed with chicken, quail and eggs, with saffron-scented creamy rice, cooked underground for several hours. Mahadaji Scindia was known to travel through the region in disguise to look into the affairs of the state and speak to his people directly. He is said to have cooked this dish at one of his disguised gatherings.

In the mid 1900s, the Scindia family's table saw Nepali culinary influences coming in due to marriage alliances. Jiwaji Rao Scindia married Rajmata Vijaya Raje, who was born and brought up in Madhya Pradesh and had a Nepalese mother and was brought up by her grandparents; so that is where the first influence of Nepali culture and cuisine came into Gwalior. Thereafter, Madhavrao Scindia II's marriage to Madhavi Raje from Nepal added more Nepali dishes to the family's cookbook. They included russ, a Nepali chicken soup, sekuwa chicken or skewered meat, and the Nepali anda, a fluffy omelette with garlic, green chillies and cheese.

These additions have now led to a menu that features a mixture of Maratha dishes, ranging from varan, pulaos, various rassas (curries) basundi, shrikhand, Gwalior's celebrated imartis, and Nepali fare like chicken badi (lotus chicken, as it opens up like a lotus once it is fried in oil and soda), bhuteko massu (mutton cooked in spices), momos and kalo dal (black dal).[39]

In the west of India too, in Rajasthan, royal culinary legacy is rich. In *Kanhadade Prabandha*, a book written by the poet Padmanabha in AD 1455 on Kanhadadeva, a ruler of Jalore, a city in Rajasthan, one can find a few mentions of food. Padmanabha shares a brief description of the royal table laden with dishes such as papad, salan, sev, suhali (crispy flour chips), manda (dumplings), khaja (a savoury snack), badi (a variety of dumpling) and lapsika (mixed grains). This was the table of a Vaishnavite ruler, different from that of a Rajput, whose meals were often laden with meat. The Rajputs commonly drank liquor and took small amounts of opium 'to heighten courage', sometimes even giving it to their horses. Their ways were different from those of the Vaishavite rulers.

Here, royal cuisine came into the spotlight around the late eighteenth and nineteenth centuries, when the prominent kingdoms of the region were formed. During Mughal rule, the Rajput rulers were granted high positions in the court, especially those who allied with the Mughals. Those kingdoms that did not accept Mughal suzerainty were constantly busy with war. Those in proximity to the Mughals had an obvious exchange of culinary notes. But if you compare the royal Rajasthani fare with that of the Mughals, you'll notice how the former doesn't even compare to the grandioseness and seriousness with which the latter viewed food. Primitive royal Rajasthani food was mostly rustic, using native ingredients that grew sparingly in this desert land. It was nothing like what you'll experience in the marvellous haveli-turned-hotels of Bikaner, Udaipur and Jaipur today.

Royal Rajasthani cuisine can broadly be divided into two types—Marwar and Mewar. Jodhpur, Jaipur, Udaipur and Bikaner were the major kingdoms of this region. The legacies of Marwari and Mewari kitchens are easily 250 to 300 years old, but a lot of written documentation is believed to have been lost during Mughal invasion, leaving little information on them. One can mostly chronicle only what it was like around 100 years ago.[40] One of the most common features of these regions is the scarce availability of food ingredients and water. So, the people relied heavily on milk, buttermilk and other dairy products to cook their dishes. The Marwar kingdom was rich, with moneylenders in the darbar, and the rajas often travelled to Delhi to mingle with the Mughals, where their cooks exchanged ideas and recipes.

Predominantly vegetarian, the royals still needed to eat meals that were textured like meat to blend in with the Mughal kings, which led to the development of recipes such as aate ki subji or chakki saag, where flour was washed to take the starch off and leave more of the gluten (a protein) in, which was then steamed to give it a meaty texture. It was served with a meaty gravy. The royal chefs came up with innovations within the predominantly vegetarian cuisine, and thus were born preparations such as gatta, or besan dumplings. Besan, or chickpea flour, makes up 60 per cent of the royal cuisine and is used in almost all forms—savoury and sweet. Although chickpea is not an indigenous Indian crop, historians believe that it may have come to India through Afghanistan (its Hindi name is Kabuli chana even today).

Food in the Mewar kingdoms was fairly different from the cuisine of Marwar. Since Mewar had more greenery, mountains and lakes, the food there also featured fish like sawal and other lake fish.

Unlike the Mughals or the Awadhis, Rajasthani kitchens didn't use whole dried fruits and nuts or saffron. In fact, it was so rustic that there is barely any early mention of expensive ingredients or desserts. For example, the popular Rajasthani dish called ghewar doesn't find mention among early royal recipes. Old Rajasthani recipes mention basic sweets, like kheer, badam halwa, til laddoo, sohan papdi, besan barfi and besan laddoo. Varq too, which is generously slathered on Rajasthani maas or ghewar these days, was used sparingly, mainly to mark a dish as safe to consume for the king.

Another commonality between the various kingdoms of Rajasthan was the consumption of wheat and bajra, and their jungle cuisine. In the early eighteenth and nineteenth centuries, when the royals were not at war, for two to three months in a row they'd set out to hunt in the wild. Each kingdom had its own speciality. Bharatpur, which had a lake, was known for its water birds nestings; the Bikaner kingdom for sandgrouse; and the hot regions of Jodhpur and Jaisalmer for their wild boar, blackbuck, quail, partridge, boar, bustard and venison. The heads of bigger animals were often brought back as trophies, and special chefs were appointed to cook birds and small animals.[41]

Before the advent of jeeps and cars, the royals travelled for shikars in their caravans with an entourage that also comprised a line of cooks. They would kill twenty to thirty animals, which would be used to cook a meal for the group. Since they travelled for longer durations, the cooks carried some ingredients along, like ghee, chillies (in abundance), rock salt and flour. The meats would be marinated in a handful of these ingredients and slow-cooked in their own juices on a spitfire, since water was too scarce to permit other methods of cooking. This jungle cuisine gave rise to popular Rajasthani dishes like khud khargosh, laal maas and hara maas. Today, these dishes are cooked using an excess of spices, and sometimes even with rich dairy and dried fruits and nuts.

A unique vegetarian jungle dish to emerge during this time was paniya batti, a dish made of 'akda', a desert cactus leaf, which was cooked in a fire created by burning cow dung cakes. The royals didn't shoot indiscriminately or during summers and monsoons, which make up the breeding season for animals. The Wildlife Protection Act of 1972 finally put an end to their pastime, and now 'jungle cuisine' is just a glamorous item in the royal cuisine repertoire, but made with market meat.

An ingredient that was used by the royals and lay people alike was kachri (an indigenous desert vegetable), which was added in marinades as it allowed the meats to break down faster. It was also eaten stir-fried by vegetarians. In the royal palaces, non-vegetarian food was often cooked outside the mahal, in an area called 'bahar ka rasoda', while vegetarian fare was cooked inside the palace, in the 'andar ka rasoda'. There is barely any written record of royal Rajput recipes, but it was the storekeepers who were in some way custodians of these recipes since they pulled out the ingredients as and when the cooks from the royal kitchen asked for them.

One defunct tradition from this region is that of making a spirit called 'ashav', which sounds like nothing less than the botanical cocktail of today. It is made by mixing together herbs, spices, fruit and 'kasturi' (a combination of saffron, dried fruit, herbs, nuts and seeds). The royals also drank something called jagmohan, a spirit of dried fruit, spices and herbs, once brewed by the princes. Production of spirits was banned in the state in 1952, but the ban was reversed in 2006.

The later Rajasthani royals had an affinity with the British and often mingled with the sahibs. They travelled extensively to Europe and acquainted themselves with its customs, traditions, educational systems and culinary habits too. This reflects in the ways of the Bikaner kingdom. The princely state was founded by Rao Bika, the oldest son of Rao Jodha, the king of Jodhpur, in 1465. Though their last three generations are predominantly vegetarian, where the mainstay was Rajasthani dishes like gatta, ker sangri, patode ki subji that was cooked in their kitchens for decades, it was the European connections that introduced them to the French style of crockery and cutlery, banquet culture, monogrammed plates, the laying of tables and dining at high tables.[42] Even today, at the royal museum in the city, you'll see old menus preserved in frames. They mention classic Continental dishes, such as 'potage a la germain', fresh pea soup; 'potage andalouse', a tomato soup; 'filet de pomfret chowder', a fish soup; and 'oeufs a la Sicilienne', or eggs Sicilian style. The meal usually started with a soup, appended with salads, an entree and something that is common in almost all menus at the museum, the *Plats de Bikaner*. This was simply the thali. Interestingly, even back then, there was the concept of eating a full-plated thali, consisting of dal, subji, roti or puris, curd, dessert and more. In an ideal example of cross-pollination of ideas, the thali would then be followed by a serving of an English-style pudding made of vermicelli, cream, custard, berries and fromage to round up the elaborate affair.[43]

In north India, the Delhi Sultanate or the Muslim kingdom held steady ground from the thirteenth to the sixteenth centuries. These rulers were Central Asian warriors who practised Islam. This long dynasty changed hands from the Mamluk, Khilji, Tughlaq, and Sayyid finally to Lodhi. During this time, Indian cuisine may have been exposed to a range of flavours and textures, mostly inspired by these rulers' Central Asian roots. In the *Bagh-o-Bahar* or *The Tales of the Four Dervishes* (a collection of stories by the poet Amir Khusro, who was the son of a Turkish officer in the service of Iltutmish, the sultan of Delhi) I struck gold with the references to the food from that Indo-Muslim culture. The merchants who come from Persia, Yemen, China and Turkey mention dishes like the fragrant yakhni pulao, made with mutton, cooked in a broth of onion, cassia leaves, black pepper and ginger. The korma pulao was made in a similar manner, but with thin slices of meat. Mutanjan pulao had kid meat, sugar and clarified butter, and was sweetened using fruits or nuts. The kuku pulao had hard-boiled eggs. The zardah was a dish of egg yolk; kaliyah consisted of meat boiled in sour milk and hot spices; and do piyazah featured meat cooked with onions.[44]

The tales describe a number of dishes, and some are exquisite, like the badami, which had flour pounded with almonds and baked; raughan josh, meat cakes cooked in ghee; and nan-i-nimat, meat fried or boiled and refried in butter, mixed with bread and baked. The kabab kofte-ke had fried lumps of pounded meat, while the kebab tikke-ke had fried balls of chopped or minced meat. Murg-ke kebab was made with fowl meat, and khaginah was a variety of omelette. A dish called malghubah has kid meat boiled in water all night long and then cooked with dried fruits and nuts such as almonds, pistachio, dates, raisins and walnuts. Shabdeg was meat and turnips cooked together overnight. Halim referred to a barley pudding cooked with milk, and harisha a liquid jelly. The ubiquitous samosa also finds a mention here, this time stuffed with spices. The book mentions a variety of breads, like paratha, shirmal, whose dough was kneaded with milk and not water, gao-didah and gao-zaban, which looked like the eye or tongue of a cow, and chau-patti, a thin cake of flour, baked and eaten with butter. Waraki is the Persian name for a paratha that has layers that peel off. There is also a sweet bread called kabuli.[45]

There is a mention of a variety of desserts, such as the firni, a preparation of rice powder (it also had a little camphor in it); shir-i birinj, another kind of rice pudding; malai, which was a name for a cream-based dessert; halwa, a pudding of butter, flour and milk; pan bhatta, a dish that was kept in water overnight and boiled the next day in fresh water; and faludah. There is also mention of tamarind sherbet, lauziyat or almond cakes, and rewris, a variety of sweetmeat.[46]

When Babur defeated Ibrahim Lodhi in the first Battle of Panipat, it was an event that marked the official end of the Delhi Sultanate and the beginning of the Mughal empire in India. Babur was succeeded by his eldest son Humayun, who was followed by Akbar, Jahangir and Shah Jahan . . . all of whom left great culinary legacies behind.

From the Rajputs to the Marathas, several Indian-origin rulers declined with the advent of the Mughals. The latter's cuisine changed the way Indian food was eaten through the centuries that followed.

The Mughal empire endured for about three hundred years and was the last of the prominent pre-modern empires in India, soon after which the British took over. At its peak, it extended over 3.2 million square kilometres, and was home to 150 million people from diverse cultures. It was one of the most powerful and culturally rich dynasties ever witnessed in the Indian subcontinent. While initially the word 'Mughal's was a Persian term for the 'uncultured' Mongols, it later came to define Babur's dynasty in India.

Since their invasion, the Mughals had settled in north India, where the Delhi Sultanate had ruled, engaging in the ways of Hindus and Muslims who were living in the country. As Muslims, the Mughals were mainly of Sunni patrilineage, but by marriage and for other reasons, Shias and Hindus also became part of their kingdom. Over the decades that the Mughals ruled India, their court developed a unique culture of its own and became a melting pot of communities—both immigrants and indigenous Indians.

The Mughals maintained a stronghold in Delhi. Since the region was bounded by the Aravalli Hills in the west and south, and by the Jamuna on the east, Delhi became a strategic spot to settle in. Delhi had a 115-mile corridor that separated it from as well as connected it to the Deccan Plateau, the Thar Desert, the Himalayas and the lush land of Punjab, and it had access to two of the most important rivers of the subcontinent— the Ganges and the Indus. And all these factors played an important role in the growth of the kingdom, its culture and subsequently its cuisine.

I have always preferred to understand the history of any region's cuisine through the historical writings from or about the region. Fortunately, there is ample Mughal literature and scores of cookbooks dedicated to their food. In books on the old Shahjahanabad, Delhi's ancient and much more romantic name, there are descriptions of old Mughal markets that bring back visions of what I had imagined an Arab marketplace would look like: something out of the tales of Aladdin, Sinbad the Sailor and other stories from the *Arabian Nights*—buzzing, dusty, canopied stalls selling grains and vegetables, and vendors roaming about with carts of kebabs being skewered and roasted on hot coals.

One of the most fascinating food-related mentions is that of the qahwa khanas, or the coffee houses, of Chandni Chowk in the eighteenth-century writings of Anand Ram Mukhlis, a lexicographer and poet from the later Mughal period. He says,

Qahwa-house is a place where people sit and make merry and drink it (coffee). Only qahwa (coffee) for qahwa-khana (coffee-house) is used in the verses of many poets. It is said that in vilayat (Middle East and Central Asia) there are numerous qahwa-houses, very elegant and graceful. High nobles go and make merry there. Meetings of men of taste, eloquent persons, poets, men like nightingales assemble there twice a day. In Shahjahanabad there are one or two shops in Chandni Chowk where the elite retire, and engage themselves in reciting poems and eloquent conversation, and take a cup of qahwa at great cost.[47]

It is apparent that this was perhaps the subcontinent's first brush with the concept of the coffee shop. In the Asian-Islamic world, qahwa houses were centres of political discourse, cultural exchange and intellectual debate, although this brew was not as potent as it was in the Arab world.

Among all the Mughal rulers that India saw, Babur's grandson Akbar can be credited with building the Mughal state as we know it, with all its grandeur and magnificence. You understand this from the pages of *Ain-i-Akbari*, the last volume of the *Akbarnama*, a conclusive work that encapsulates Akbar's reign. The *Ain-i-Akbari* gives us a glimpse into Mughal kitchens, or the matbakh, like no other book from the era does. From this we know that the imperial palace had separate cooking areas for men and women. The zenana kitchen or the 'female cooking area' was separated from the mardana kitchen or the 'male cooking area', and food was transferred between the two by the eunuchs. There was also a beverages and food storage area called abdar khana. The *Ain-i-Akbari* mentions the prices of food items in the bazaar during that period. In one chapter (*Ain-i matbakh*) Abul Fazl, the writer, delves into the role of food in an emperor's life.[48]

His Majesty brings his foresight to bear even on this (kitchen) department, and has given many wise regulations for it; nor can reason be given why he should not do so, as the equilibrium of temperament (i'tidāl-i mizāj), the strength of the body (tawānā'ī-i tan), the capability of receiving external and internal grace, and the acquisition of worldly and religious advantages, depend ultimately on proper care being shown for appropriate (munāsib) food. This knowledge distinguishes man from beasts, with whom, as far as mere eating is concerned, he stands upon the same level. If his Majesty did not possess so lofty a mind, so great a comprehension, so universal a kindness, he would have chosen the path of solitude, and given up sleep and food altogether. Even now, when he has taken upon himself the temporal and spiritual leadership of the people, the question, 'what dinner has been prepared today?' never passes his tongue. In the course of twenty-four hours his Majesty eats but once, and leaves off before he is fully satisfied. Neither is there any fixed time for his meal, but the servants have always things so far ready, that in the space of an hour after the order has been given, a hundred dishes are served up . . . [49]

On any given day, Akbar had more than a hundred dishes and forty courses presented to him. Food was brought to the emperor sealed to ensure it wasn't poisoned, and this seal was only broken at his table. A line of servants, the master of the household, a few eunuchs and serving girls would hover around while he ate, which was never with the ladies of the house, who had their own special provisions for dining (though

Babur shared a meal with his sister Khadija Begam, as reported in *Baburnama*).[50] Akbar generally dined in private, except on days of public banquet, and preferred to sit on silken rugs and cushions. The food at palace meals was highly refined and the cooking was outsourced to professional cooks. However, on special occasions, the ladies of the palace took an interest in cooking. This was especially true of Nur Jahan, who was reputed to have keen interest in recipe development and in serving food.

Abul Fazl says:

Cooks from all countries (*pazandagān-i har kishwar*) prepare a variety of dishes from all kinds of grains, vegetables, meats, oils, sweets and carrots (or potherbs) 72 of various colours. Everyday such dishes are prepared as the notables (*buzurgān*) can scarcely command at their feasts, from which you can infer how exquisite the dishes which are prepared for his Majesty.[51]

The emperor spent around one thousand rupees each day to meet the expenses of the kitchen. His food and beverages were stored in a designated space, and a separate bakery called rikabkhana doled out a variety of breads for him. There was the maywa khana for fruits and a separate section to supply the emperor with cold water and drinks through the day. The main kitchen was placed around the courtyard so that it was located between the indoors and outdoors. The Mughals had a separate kitchen for the palace staff.

There were dining halls for functions located at the centre of the palace, richly decorated with murals and depictions of hunting scenes as well as battle and court scenes.[52]

Meals in the royal household were served on a 'chandni', white sheets on which the food was laid out. Each meal began with the chanting of 'Bismillah-e-rehman-e-rahim', which means 'In the name of Allah, the most beneficent and the most merciful', and usually those words were delicately embroidered on the chandni.

In Mughal cookbooks, one finds mention of dishes such as the khichri (a dish of rice and pulses, often topped with dried fruits), but more on that later. There is also mention of dopiyaza, a dish cooked without spices or be-masalih, flavoured with onion, naan and raan (cut of meat from between the buttocks and knee of an animal). The chefs had such refined skills that they coloured dishes using vegetables and fruit juices; they used saffron, fragrant flowers, aromatics and herbs like mint, dill, rose, orange blossom, fennel and basil to flavour the food; and a simple thing such as curd was turned into raitas by adding fruits and fragrant herbs.[53]

However, the Mughals didn't always eat in such a sophisticated manner. During Babur's time in India, food was still predominantly inspired by their time in Central Asia and Afghanistan. But as they began to settle more and more in the land, their cuisine expanded to include Indian-style meals, with heavy influences from Turkey and Iran.

The Mughals taught us a variety of culinary techniques and dishes. One of them is the fine art of making pulao.

Though a version of pulao also finds mention in early Tamil literature between the third and sixth centuries, to eat rice in such a refined manner is something we learnt from the well-travelled cookbooks of the Mughals.[54] Refined rice-based dishes served during the Mughal era, like moti pulao, narangi pulao, mutanjan pulao and muesseh pulao became perfect illustrations of Indo-Islamic culture. We also saw glimpses of such dishes during the time of the Delhi Sultanate. But, it was the Mughals who taught us all about cooking with fruits, often using them with meats like lamb, something that was unknown to Indians until then. A variety of Mughal breads also came to the fore during this period. In India, leavened bread-making technically started when the Portuguese landed in Goa and brought with them their pao-making skills. But the Mughals brought their unleavened flat breads, like their flaky bakarkhani, the rumali roti and shirmal, centuries before.

They also taught us the famous dum-pukht style of cooking, the slow-cooking of meats and vegetables in a sealed cauldron; the smoking of meats; the yakhni style of gravy; and the mixing of minced or ground meat and shaping it on skewers to make kebabs, which they may have learnt from their interactions with the Turks. Mughal food was cooked in copper vessels, eaten from gold or silver utensils, and the meals were either cooked in harvested rain or river water, never water from stagnant waterbodies. Akbar is, in fact, known to have imported water all the way from the Ganges because he did not like the taste of well water. He endorsed the purity and taste of the water from the river and called it the source or life or ab-e-hayat. While travelling, he had water sealed in jars delivered to him from Saran, the city on the Ganges closest to Agra. Muhammad ibn Tughluq, the sultan of the Tughlaq dynasty, also used to get water from the Ganges procured daily and brought all the way to his capital.[55]

One of the most popular stories from the Mughal kitchens is that of the origin of chaats. Because, really, what is Indian cuisine without its chutney-painted chaats? The story goes that once when Emperor Shah Jahan fell ill, a royal hakim advised him to eat food loaded with spices to strengthen his immunity. The palace khansama came up with chaat, a dish that was light on the stomach but tasty at the same time.[56] There is also another story about how chaat was invented, and you can decide which one works better for you. During the Mughal period, a canal (perhaps the Yamuna river) supplying water to the local homes was polluted, and the court hakim advised that the only way to beat this is was to urge locals to cook using a lot of healing herbs and spices like tamarind, coriander and mint.[57] I feel these are just tales, since some version of dahi vada can be traced back all the way to *Manasollasa*, which mentions the existence of dishes that combined vadas, *purikas* (similar to the puris of pani puris or papadis), curd, and a variety of spices.[58] Though chaats may have been well defined during the Mughal period, they existed in various forms earlier too.

Ideas flowed in the opposite direction too. Certain Indian dishes like bharta, poori and besan roti, which were not part of the Mughal repertoire, were picked from native Indian kitchens and the Mughals' interactions with other Indian royalty. The other things picked up by the Mughals was the use of betel leaves, mustard oil, mishri, multani mitti, mahua, sandalwood and batasha—all of which found ample usage in the Mughal kitchen.

One prominent dish from this time is the khichuri. It is believed that the Mughals fell in love with it during their time here. In fact, it was one of Akbar's favourite dishes. When they employed Brahmin cooks in their kitchens, they brought with them typical Indian dishes like the khichuri. The imperial kitchen completely reinvented the humble khichuri, with additions of refined ingredients like musk, rose water, spices like nutmeg, dried fruits like raisin, saffron, basanta flowers and edible silver foil. The European traveller Alexander Hamilton, who spent around thirty-five years as a trader and spoke several Asian languages, says in one of his accounts that Aurangzeb especially liked his khichuri with a pickle or salted fish on the side. Jahangir in *Tuzuk* (his memoir) describes a khichuri made of bajra and peas, which he tasted in Gujarat, as laziza (meaning delicious).[59]

While they got acquainted with some spices during their time here, the Mughals taught us how to use them sparingly to create refined dishes. In the Mughal cookbooks you'll find mention of pepper, cardamom, coriander seeds, cinnamon, cloves and fresh ginger. But there is little mention of garlic and turmeric. The chilli was completely missing—it arrived in India only in the sixteenth century with the Portuguese. You'll find mention of chillies only around the mid-eighteenth century, as mirch-i surkh. One example of their use was in a chilli chutney, in a cookbook called *Risala Dar Bayan-i At'ima.*[60]

Unlike the other royals discussed in this chapter, the Mughals had a knack for cataloguing recipes in their cookbooks. Several journals, like the *Ain-i-Akbari, Alawan-e-Nemat* and *Nuskha-e-Shahjahani,* throw light on the great Mughal kitchen. These hand-written Persian manuscripts begin with no date of compilation, nor the name of the compiler. For example, *Nuksha-e-Shahjahani* was put together during the reign of emperor Shah Jahan, maybe written by one of the cooks of the royal kitchen.

In *Ain-i-Akbari* one finds mention of twenty-five kinds of grains, twenty vegetables, sixteen spices, twelve types of rice, thirty-seven varieties of pickles, and ten types of sheep and goat meat, such as Afghani, Kashmiri and Hindustani. The Mughal meal was predominantly non-vegetarian. They also ate game birds like partridge, bustard and fowl, as well as venison. Poultry was reared separately for the emperor's table, and the birds were hand-fed breadcrumbs seeped in saffron and rosewater, and massaged with oil and musk. Surprisingly, beef is not mentioned at all. In fact, Humayun stopped eating beef after the killing of cows was condemned by the Hindus of the region, while Akbar imposed restrictions on cow slaughter. The emperor personally observed meatless days. Abul Fazl tells us:

Whenever long fasts are ended, the first dishes of meat come dressed from the apartments of Maryam Makānī (Ḥamīda Bānū Begam, Akbar's mother), after that from the other begams, the princes, and select intimates (barkhī nazdīkān).[61]

Akbar's practice of meatless days was also adopted by Jehangir, but the latter's successors were less enthusiastic about all-vegetarian meals, though cow slaughter prohibitions continued. Charity through food distribution was common. For their meatless days, the Mughals developed many vegetarian dishes; they relished saags, ate pickled tender bamboo shoot and kachnar, and savoured a variety of bhartas—a dish of mashed vegetables like eggplant and gourd, roasted to gain a smoky flavour.

Another well-written cookbook is the *Ni'matnama,* written in Naksh, a cursive Arabic script, during Ghiyath Shah's reign and added to by his son Nasir Shah, ruler of the independent Malwa sultanate. This particular sultanate had a Turkic origin and settled in the central part of India, which is present-day Madhya Pradesh. During his time, there were Central Asian influences pouring into Indian cuisine. The book was written in the early sixteenth century, in a combination of Urdu and Farsi. The range of recipes included karhi, a curd-based dish which had chickpea flour; khichuri, discussed earlier; piccha, a dish made with the water left over from cooking rice and grain; bhrat, or mashed vegetable; phat, or split pulses; khandawi, swollen parched grains; breads like puri and chapati; bhuji or fried vegetables; achar; rabari, which was thickened and sweetened milk; phini, a fried sweet made of flour; khaja, a dish made with sweet milk; khir or kheer; paliv or pulao; sikh, skewered meat, fish or seekh; yakhni; shurba, which was a kind of soup; kebab; kofta; halwa made of flour, honey and water; bara, or fried cakes made of pulses or chickpeas; and sanbusa (fried pastries). Besides, the book contains recipes for distillation of essences and perfumes, and for concocting aphrodisiacs and remedies using ingredients such as gum, resin, fruit, leaves, barks, flower pollen, nuts and kernels.

The Ni'matnama speaks of a variety of meats, like sheep, beef, rabbit, partridge, quail, kid, chicken and pigeon. Very interesting flavours, such as camphor, musk, rose water and even ambergris (a substance produced in the gut of sperm whales, that was used as a culinary item) were used. The book not only teaches one how to cook, but also details the medicinal values of certain foods, and warns against the mixing of incompatible ingredients, like fish and milk, or curd and aubergine.[62]

One of the most interesting dishes that I found there is this book's namesake, the sambusak–sambusa–samusa. Back then, the fried flour pasties resembling the current-day samosas were stuffed with a variety of meats, like beef and venison. But Shah's version was an even more elaborate preparation of minced meat mashed with fennel, cumin, salt, cloves, coriander seeds, musk, rose water, ginger root and onions, folded into a triangular parcel, skewered and fried in sweet-tasting ghee.

Interestingly, the sanbusa is a common dish found in various cookbooks of Asian, Islamic and Iranian lineage, and the predecessor of the great Indian samosa. It is named after samsa, the Central Asian pyramidal pastries, and has been referred to as sanbusak, sanbusaq or even sanbusaj over the centuries in various books.

For me, it was an appropriate dish after which to title my book. This seemingly Indian dish has travelled far and wide before it became a mainstay in our gullies. The first mention of samosa can be found around the tenth or eleventh century in the Middle East, in historian Abolfazl Beyhaqi's work *Tarikh-e Beyhaghi*, where it is referred to as sambosa. In its original form, as made in the kitchens of the Ghaznavid empire, samosas were pastries filled with meat and dried fruit and then deep fried. We don't know when exactly it assumed its current form, filled with simply minced meat or potatoes and peas.[63] But we do know that when Akbar annexed the Malwa Sultanate in 1562 CE, the *Ni'mmatnama* was procured by the Mughals, and subsequently by the sultanate's kitchens too.[64]

A dish from within the Mughal court itself that caught my fancy was the bughra. This is mentioned in the accounts of Bayazid Bayat, one of the members of the royal court and a historian from Humayun's period. Bughra is a vegetable stew eaten with noodles.[65] It is perhaps an interesting nook in which to establish the shared history of vermicelli, noodles and spaghetti, a history that spans the Indian subcontinent, Central Asia, China and Italy.

A culinary subject from the Mughal courtroom that deserves a chapter of its own is their fascination with fruits. They took fruits very seriously and cultivated elaborate orchards. Starting with Babur, the Mughals, who tremendously missed their homeland and the fruits that it bore, brought with them a fruit-eating culture. Their orchards were the pride of their palaces, and some rulers like Akbar even got horticulturists from different parts of the world to take care of their fruit gardens. In *Ain-i-Akbari*, Abul Fazl writes:

> His Majesty looks upon fruits as one of the greatest gifts of the Creator, and pays much attention to them. The horticulturalists of Iran and Turan have, therefore, settled here, and the cultivation of trees is in a flourishing state. Melons and grapes have become very plentiful and excellent; and water-melons, peaches, almonds, pistachios, pomegranates are everywhere to be found.

This was the period when many new varieties of fruits were being introduced in India. Jahangir appreciated his father's efforts and says: '. . . during the reign of his Majesty Arsh Āshyānī (Akbar), most fruits of the wilāyat that were not in India were introduced.' He notes that melons, mangoes and other fruits of good quality were grown in Agra and its vicinity, and adds that several thousand ananas (pineapple) were annually cultivated in Agra's Gulafshan garden. There is also mention of a drink made with watermelon (tarbuz) flavoured with rose and a little sugar candy.

Fruits not only had cultural value, they had political significance too, especially if they were from foreign lands, and were used as gifts. The gifting and sharing of food items were trends from the reign of Babur to that of Humayun. The Mughal courts had rituals where sugar and fruit were sent to call for a truce. Meat hunted by the emperor was another food gift, which had a great value since it was the emperor who decided to share it.

The Mughal traits of serving, sharing and gifting food are the culmination of a lifestyle they may have picked up from other cultures like the Timurid, Persian and Iranian, where a special 'farman' was issued in a courtroom for food arrangements to be made for guests. That, mixed with the Indian art of guest reception, led to a culture steeped in hospitality.

Besides being particular about their ingredients and etiquette, the Mughals indulged in a bit of exquisite food vocabulary. Take, for instance, the word za'iqa—it had great significance, especially for Jahangir, whose attention to detail and love for food were legendary. Jahangir was fond of mangoes, and on one occasion spoke about how mangoes were only kept in the royal storage. They were brought in from the Deccan, Burhanpur, Gujarat and the Malwa countryside. He observed how some of them had less stringy or fibrous flesh than others; and talks of their juiciness or khwushabi, their tastiness or lazzat-u-chashni, and their digestibility or kam siqli. He claimed that the mangoes of Chapramau in Agra were better than mangoes from any other area of Hindustan. In one instance, he comments on Persian apples being better than Indian ones.

Dried fruits and nuts also had an important place in Mughal kitchens. The Mughals were perhaps the first importers of almonds, pistachios, walnuts, dried apricots, plums and raisins in India. The produce came from Central Asia and Persia along the new roads that had been constructed to facilitate trade throughout northern India, Central Asia and Persia. The Mughals snacked on them and also added them to savoury dishes, as mentioned earlier. The Mughals ate two large meals in a day—one at 11 a.m. and another at sunset; these usually ended with a session of hookah and paan.[66]

Interestingly, their ways affected a very unlikely community from Rajasthan/Gujarat—the Pushtimargi Vaishnavas. The age of Vithalnathji (the founder of this community) was at its pinnacle in the early Mughal era, and the effects of the latter can be seen in the Pushtimargi Vaishnavas' luxurious lifestyle choices that may have mimicked the Mughal–Rajput way of life. Mughal motifs are reflected in their arts and crafts, and in the adornments, especially the robes and jewellery, offered to their deities like Shrinathji, Shri Yamunaji and Lord Krishna, and especially in the robes, jewellery, and attire of the community's acharyas or gurus like Vithalnathji and Shrihariraiji. A Mughal-Iranian influence can even be seen in the very idea of chhappan bhog, the idea of serving before the Lord a spread of fifty-six food items.[67]

After the Mughals, an offshoot of Indian cuisine developed with the Awadhi influence. Awadh can be described as the region extending from Faizabad to Lucknow; it was once a province of the Mughal empire, but the state became an independent authority in the reign of their first nawab, Shuja-ud-Daula, who ruled from AD 1753 to AD 1775.[68] Naturally, a lot of their cuisine was inspired by the Mughal kitchens, since they were closely connected. And like the Mughal royals, the Awadhis were influenced by Turkish and Arabic cuisines; in fact, the impact of Persian cuisine was more, considering they were predominantly Shia Muslims.

Awadh did not have access to the sea or a port, so the main source of income for the palace was land revenue. Its fertile plains were lush with crops like wheat, rice, millets, maize, pulses, mustard seed for oil, and opium in some parts.[69] The Awadhis also tended to a large number of mango orchards producing several varieties of mangoes, the leading one being the dussehri aam. They didn't pay their dues to the Mughal empire after becoming independent, so the wealth stayed with the nawabs and they grew richer by the day. Obviously, a lavish lifestyle and refined cuisine followed. We know that Shuja-ud-Daula spent Rs 60,000 every month on kitchen expenses alone.[70]

Like in an urban restaurant kitchen, the staff had a definitive hierarchy, with a sculler to do the dishes and separate staff at different stations that took care of the grinding, chopping, frying and other kitchen work. Work was specialized: there were rice specialists, and separate specialists for naan, desserts, korma, pulaos and so on. The food for the staff and the court members would be cooked by a bawarchi and the naan baai (bread maker), both of whom cooked in bulk. A 'rakabdar' made food in smaller quantities, mainly for the nawab and his entourage.

The Awadhs didn't eat at low tables. They ate out of a dastarkhan, which had various 'khans' or trays filled with food. The chefs would send the food to the nawab in something called a 'tora', and each tora would have multiple 'khans' that made the dastarkhan. Each tora would also be sealed with a special marking so the nawab could be assured that the food wasn't tampered with, on the way from the kitchen to the dastarkhan. A well-done dastarkhan would often feature dishes similar to those of the Mughal spread, but these were even more refined. A sample dastarkhan might have a mutanjan (a rice dish cooked with meat), muzaffar (rice dish cooked with fruits, nuts and meat), sevaiyan ka muzaafar (a dish made of vermicelli) and breads like sheermal, made not just with flour and milk, but also with cream, sugar and ghee, and painted with saffron. The Awadhis took immense pride in their pulaos, which ranged from the simple parboiled-rice-combined-with-meat variety, to the safeda, which had fried vegetables. Rice and bread were eaten with kormas, thick curries dotted with nuts; kaliyas, which were thinner curries flavoured with turmeric; and salan, a curry with vegetables.

While a lot of these preparations featured in the Mughal kitchen too, what separates the Awadhi kitchen is that they seldom used whole spices. Masalas were finely ground, and the Awadhi curries were silken-smooth, often strained through a muslin cloth. The addition of edible fragrances was another typical Awadhi feature. The royal meals were flavoured with a meetha itr made from florals, screwpine (kewra) or roses. Theirs was one of the few kitchens in India where bread was made in a metal tandoor, as opposed to the clay one that Indians had been using for centuries.

A typical royal Awadhi kitchen used ingredients such as poppy seeds, chironji, garam masalas like mace and cinnamon, and khoya instead of paneer. Vegetables, such as eggplant, gourd, turai, peas, cabbage, arbi and potato found a footing here. There was liberal use of saffron, nuts, itr and silver and gold varq. An interesting feature was the lazzat-e taam, their secret spice blend of twenty-seven to thirty-two spices, which was used in their savoury preparations.

The Awadhis had chefs and karigars brought down from Central Asia, and the cuisine saw numerous foreign influences too. The addition of itr and the use of saffron may be a Persian trait. One of their preparations, dulma, seems to have been influenced by the Turkish dolma, except that this one isn't stuffed vine leaves but a variety of stuffed vegetables (mainly tomato and bitter gourd). Meat was often from goat and cattle, and many recipes were dictated by the hakims, who ensured that the flavours and ingredients were balanced based on their innate properties, such as by ensuring that ingredients with heating and cooling properties were used in the right proportions, keeping in mind whom the food was meant for. Warriors might be served food that would enhance their strength, and men were given food to enhance their virility.

In the heart of the subcontinent, another royal line that branched out from the Mughals were the nawabs of Bhopal. They were Muslim rulers who first served under the Mughal empire and independently thereafter. This royal house is special because many women rulers/begums came to the fore during this period. The first of the Bhopali rulers was Qudsia Begum, who ruled from AD 1819 until AD 1837, followed by Sikander Begum from AD 1837 to AD 1868, and lastly Shahjahan Begum, from AD 1868 to AD 1901. It was Shahjahan Begum who had a deep love for the good life and an interest in the development of regional cuisine. From clothes to culinary flair, a cultural renaissance took place in the royal family of Bhopal under her rule. A stellar feature was the dynasty's celebration of the turn of seasons. The celebrations were named after colours: Jashn Hariyali, Jashn Gulabi, Jashn Firoza and so on. The food items served during those celebrations were also dedicated to a particular colour. The colour was reflected in the crockery used, the décor and the clothes of the people in the court. Many of the recipes developed as part of these seasonal menus form the core of Bhopali royal cuisine. They are popular even today; for example, the well-known Bhopali rizala, a dish of chicken in a thick gravy of blended masalas and meat cooked with large amounts of coriander leaves, was developed during Jashn Hariyali for its green colour.[71]

Since the roots of Bhopali royal lineage lie not in Persia or Turkey but in Afghanistan, their recipes showcased different culinary practices from Delhi and Awadh. Unlike the recipes used in refined Mughal kitchen, Bhopali kitchens used those inherited from their Afghani ancestors. This cuisine wasn't as finely tuned as Awadhi, or as robust as Hyderabadi, but lay somewhere in between. The typical dishes included sheer korma, mainly cooked during Eid, which didn't have any seviyan, using instead lots of dried fruit (a typical Afghani touch), along with concentrated milk and malai. They also made something called the sheer using thin seviyan, and a Bhopali-style firni, which had very little rice and was strained through mulmul cloth before being served. The royal begums seldom ate vegetables and mainly relied on shikar meat, such as venison, or goat, chicken or fish. But as a mark of respect towards the Hindus of the region, the royal court didn't serve beef, and the Eid qurbanis were marked by sacrificing either a camel or a horse instead of cattle.[72]

A unique Muslim royal house that merged the northern and southern royal lineages was the Qutb Shahi dynasty. They were a combination of Deccan (Telugu culture) and Muslim royal lineage. Their ancestors were vassals to the Sultanate in Baghdad and belonged to the Turkic Qara Qoyunlu tribe, which controlled parts of Iraq, Armenia and Azerbaijan. Hyderabad was a place of pride for this dynasty in India, and there lived many foreigners, including Persians, Arabs, Turks, Burmese and, much later, even Portuguese. Around 1687, the Qutb Shahis were defeated by the Mughals, who sent a viceroy to rule their land. The viceroy's successor became the first Nizam ul Mulk, followed by six nizams leading up to the current one.

The food of the royal family of Hyderabad was also influenced by the Mughals. Mixed marriages in the family meant that there was Turkish influence in the food and some Andhra influences as well. The Mughals did not like spicy food but the south Indians did, which made Hyderabadi Muslim food a spicier version of Mughal food. It was, therefore, a combination of several styles of cooking and included spicy biryanis, succulent kebabs, the flavour of curry leaves, the bite of beans and greens, the sour tang of tamarind, cooling raitas and the sharpness of chillies. The Nizami cuisine catalogues a variety of dishes you wouldn't ordinarily find in Mughal cookbooks, like chippe ka gosht, meat cooked in a chippa or an earthenware cooking pot, and pathar ke gosht, meat cooked on hot stone. The aloo ke garlay is a dish strikingly similar to the batata wada of Maharashtra. Then there is garelu, or deep-fried dal vadas; their safed mirchi ka salan has south Indian hints of dry coconut; and the chepala pulusu, i.e., curry is an Andhra-style tamarind-based fish soup.

This is also the region that popularized the Indian dish halim, a variety of the Arab harissa, where lentils and wheat are cooked with meat and served with a scattering of deep-fried brista. This dish in India originated from the Nizam's palace. His Yemeni guards ate it during the nineteenth century, and it is also the first non-vegetarian dish to get a Geographical Identification tag in India.[73] Technically a staff meal, the haleem got fine-tuned in the royal kitchens and was mainly eaten during Ramadan. Like the Mughals, the Nizams too liked their khichuri, and theirs came teeming with meat and a dried-fruit-and-nut paste, among other ingredients.

The rule of the Muslims in India, especially of the Mughals, was at its zenith from AD 1750 to AD 1857, when they began to lose power to the British.

On the east coast of India, one of the largest royal states among the Eastern States Agency (a grouping of princely states) in British India was Mayurbhanj in Odisha. It is Odisha's largest district and is named after the two medieval ruling families of the region—the Mayuras and Bhanjas.

Their menu featured a motley of sturdy underdog vegetables, such as the pumpkin, brinjal, potato and a wide variety of local gourds and their flowers, roots, stems and tubers. In Odisha, rice was the staple, which it is even today, and millets and maize made brief appearances in the royal kitchen. Since the state has a rich coastline, the meals there often featured a variety of fish and seafood, especially crabs, all beautifully turned into curries, stir fries and fritters (their version of deep-fried pakoras).

An iconic dish that came down from the time of the Mauryas to present-day Odisha is the mudhi mansa. Mudhi refers to puffed rice, commonly known as muri in Bengali homes, and mansa refers to meat. This dish is said to have emerged in the military corridors of the Mauryan dynasty, one of the foremost ruling dynasties of this region, and was a favourite of Emperor Ashoka. Mudhi mansa's history in Odisha goes back to the days of the wars between the Mughals and the Bhanja kings in the fourteenth and fifteenth centuries. This dish provided a filling combination of carbs and protein and was used by the kings to feed their battle-weary soldiers to provide them with strength.

The recipe was passed down from the Mauryan courts to the Kalingas, who came next, and just like that it became a staple Odiya dish. Essentially a tender mutton curry, it is cooked with onions, chillies and a bit of coriander, all served with mudhi. The Mayurbhanj kings who came later had their own rendition, where shikar meat was used in place of mutton in the dish. This preparation continues to be cooked in the royal palace even today, although the meat now comes from the market.

Many stand-out recipes come from the traditional cuisine of this region, and are relevant even today. One such is pakhala, derived from overnight fermentation of rice and water. A typical summer-time meal, it is served with some green chilli, onion, curd and other condiments that add flavour to the otherwise tepid preparation. What I find most interesting is that pakhala is similar to pazhan kanji of Kerala, which is also eaten with an add-on of coconut chutneys and kandhari, or bird's eye chillies. There are versions of this preparation in Andhra Pradesh, Gujarat and Odisha too.

Besides, there was palau and khichdis made of rice cooked with meat, as well as rice cooked with lentils. Dalma is a dish of lentils cooked with vegetables, and what separates it from dal in other parts of the country is the addition of chopped vegetables like raw papaya and banana, eggplant and pumpkin that add a bite. Their menu also featured a variety of stir-fries, like alu potala rasa, a dish of potato and parval (pointed gourd), kadali manja rai, made of banana stem with a splattering of mustard, and besara, which has deep notes of mustard paste.

The most beautiful aspect of Odisha's cuisine is that there isn't a drastic difference between the meals of the royals and the commoners, both of whom have predominantly relied on the local flora and fauna for nourishment.

We have now covered some of the larger culinary influences that have impacted Indian cuisine and added on to its thick culinary fabric. While India has always had a rich heritage of royalty, more than I can cover in one chapter, the influences mentioned here do paint a vivid picture of how various dynasties and their cuisines led up to the next stage of Indian cuisine.

4

TRADERS AND CONQUERORS

If it wasn't for travel and trade, pepper and turmeric wouldn't have made their way outside the Indian subcontinent, and chilli and chai wouldn't have come in. Although I secretly wish turmeric had not gone out and become this snob of a super food that it has, and that pineapple, coffee and guava had come in much earlier. Imagine, our Harappan ancestors didn't get to taste the sweet-sour notes of the pineapple or get to gather their yams and wild rice after an energizing cup of coffee or cacao.

Whether it was the fourth century BC, the period of the *Jataka Tales* or the fifteenth century AD, when *The Arabian Nights* was written—trade, travel and adventure have been recurring themes in all depictions of the Indian subcontinent and in our own stories and folklore. The fact that researchers have found old Mesopotamian coins on the subcontinent and Harappan coins in Mesopotamia, two of the oldest civilizations in the world, proves how cross-continental trade went hand in hand as humans evolved.

Historically, travellers and merchants spurred a greater production and availability of resources. The routes they chose for trading impacted the social, political and culinary histories of their reign, and of the regions in which they traded. Take the example of the chilli: To think of it not as our own but as something that was imported only a little over 450 years ago is both shocking and humbling. But the truth remains that even an ingredient that is so widely assumed to be Indian only made an appearance in Indian kitchens around 1542 in the Malabar region, thanks to foreign travellers or traders. Although the chilli per se is an ancient crop, with accounts of it dating as far back as 7500 BC in South America (which predates the Indus Valley civilization), it was only thousands of years later that it made it to India. But more on this historical spice later.[1]

Understanding the role of merchants was important for me to determine how the Indian pantry gained access to foreign ingredients. Perhaps what miso, gochujang and truffle oil are for us now is what cinnamon, rose and pineapple were for Indians back then.

Popular history has us believe that it was the Portuguese explorer Vasco da Gama, who, on his visit to India around AD 1498, opened the gates of Indo-European trade and travel; but this is far from the truth. Accounts of foreigners visiting the Indian subcontinent go as far back as the fifth and sixth centuries BC. When visiting Europeans went back home after years of weary travel, they spoke of India as nothing less than an enchanted land, full of secrets, spices, colours (and, of course) elephants. This attracted more men from Europe to visit the subcontinent.

One of the foremost European travellers was Eudoxus, who came to India from Cyzicus (an ancient city in Turkey) in 118 BC via a coastal route of around 5,000 miles. Others followed suit. Scylax, a sea captain and Greek explorer, set off from Caryanda, an ancient city in Anatolia, Greece, reaching the shores of the Indus and sailing down the river to India, on the decree of the Achaemenid emperor Darius I (he himself had come all the way to the subcontinent before the Exodus). Historian Hecataeus from Miletus (another ancient Greek city), visited India around 500 BC, and so did a physician named Ctesias.[2]

Taking the early accounts of several Greek travellers, a writer called Herodotus compiled them in a book named, not too innovatively, as *The Histories*.[3] The book, written on rustic papyrus scrolls, is of about 700 pages, and had a lot to say about India. Herodotus was probably one of the first Western observers to do a systematic analysis of the subcontinent, and while today very little is available of his descriptions, we know that he wrote about India as a land of raw fish and meat eaters (How very Kyoto, no?). He also pointed out that there were others practising vegetarianism and that millets existed way before wheat and rice did.

II.100: They refuse to put any live animal to death, they sow no corn, and have no dwelling-houses. Vegetables are their only food. There is a plant which grows wild in their country, bearing seed, about the size of millet-seed, in a calyx: their wont is to gather this seed and having boiled it, calyx and all, to use it for food . . . [4]

The Greeks had learnt to harness the seasonal winds of the Indian Ocean and sail across the Arabian Sea directly from Bab el Mandeb, a strait located between Yemen on the Arabian Peninsula and Djibouti in Africa, leading towards the Indian subcontinent.

The Europeans had always been fascinated with the food ingredients from this distant land. In *Questions of Milinda (Milinda-Pañha)*, a Buddhist text from the late second century BC, a dialogue between the Buddhist sage Nāgasena and an Indo-Greek king Milinda brings us to an interesting recipe.[5] The king asks the sage about a sauce made of curd, cumin, ginger and pepper. This is perhaps one of the earliest iterations of the great Indian kadhi.

While we are on the subject of Greek travellers and invaders, we must refer to the one who centuries later opened the floodgates for Indo-European interaction—Alexander, the king of Macedon in northern Greece. His kingdom was at that time one of the largest in the world, stretching from Greece to north-western India. As his troops travelled further towards the east from their land, they feared leaving their homeland and culture too far behind. And so, they began setting up colonies and cities in strategic places along the way. These cities were spots from where the armies gathered their supplies and availed amenities while he continued to conquer lands. What started off as centres for the Greek to preserve their own culture and ensure they weren't entirely cut off from the West turned out to be important points from where world culture began to be shared and borrowed.

Alexander's invasion of India in 326 BC was one of the first real trysts between Indians and Greeks. His army invaded India by crossing the Indus river and moving towards Taxila, a buzzing point of trade on the subcontinent, where the Indian king Porus, who ruled the kingdom between the Jhelum and Chenab rivers, met them in battle. This was the first time the Greeks had fought against elephants, an animal they had never seen before. While Porus's army lost the battle, Alexander still let him continue to rule under his suzerainty, a policy he followed in several other territories that he conquered between Greece and India.[6]

During this period, and after Alexander's death, several Hellenistic colonies, like Alexandria in Egypt, Antioch in Syria and Seleucia in Baghdad, cropped up. These then became channels for trade, art, culture and cuisine to move from one part of the world to another, and allowed for the Greeks and Easterners to adapt to or learn each others' customs, rituals and ways of life. Alexander not only opened up the West to the East, and vice versa, but he also started what can be called an early wave of immigration. To my dismay, however, the gyro still didn't make it to India.

To understand what Indian food was like back when early European invasions began on the subcontinent, the observations made by Alexander's comrades come in handy.

One such comrade was Aristobulus of Kassandra, a friend of Alexander's father King Philip, who accompanied him on his wars. He observed that the region (the Indian subcontinent and the Middle East) was a land of banana trees, jackfruit and asafoetida, and that the people here ate too much rice. He talks of 'a strange plant that stands in water, abundant cakes of sesame and honey'. Nearchus, one of Alexander's officers, talks about a tree generating honey without the use of bees (sugarcane) on the banks of the Hydaspes (the Roman name for the Jhelum) and of the land having abundant medicinal plants. Similarly, Greek writer Onesicritus speaks of nard, a Himalayan plant.[7]

One of the most charming visions of the Indian markets of the time is given by Periplus, a Greek coastal guide from the same period. He describes the area around Madurai as a thriving marketplace that sold Mediterranean merchandise and Indian products alike.[8] It made me picture bazaars brimming with Greek pearls and Indian pepper next to each other.

This does not mean that a bunch of travellers went from one place to another. But, during this time, a large number of Westerners left behind their imprint in the form of their culture, language, food habits, social rituals and even their gene pool, as they migrated over the years. It was perhaps the first time in history that this process was taking place at such a rapid pace and wide scale on the Indian subcontinent.

Over the next centuries, it became common for traders and travellers from Europe to reach as far as India, Arabia and

Africa using these routes. They especially came in search of novelty goods, travelling mostly in caravans, and preferred to deal with light luxury items as opposed to bulky products that would be difficult to carry back. In this way started the trading of silk, spices, ivory, gems and exotic animals—items that would fetch high value back home in Europe. Thus were born the Silk and Spice Routes, paths that connected the East to the West via the sea and over land.

Understanding these spice routes especially puts the evolution of flavours into perspective. And not just in terms of Indian cuisine but also with respect to global tastes, and how they evolved and adapted as more and more ingredients began to seep into the markets in India and everywhere else. It was this transfer of grains and food ingredients that allowed the populations—and their cuisines—to flourish in Europe and Asia.

It is the deft use of spices that distinguishes Indian cuisine from most Western cuisines. A spice is typically a sweet-smelling aromatic part of a plant. And just as they are the first ingredients to go into the kadai in the making of most Indian preparations, in terms of trade too, spices were the first among food products to stir up global networks and economies, and trigger the meshing of cultures and cuisines.

Let us first start to understand the role of the Silk Route. It begins in China (Xi'an) and moves through India, going up to Mesopotamia, Egypt, the African continent, Greece, Rome and Britain. (The use of silk as a textile originated in China around 2,700 BC and gained popularity under the Han

Dynasty. Over the years the Chinese gained monopoly over the production of the material, which they soon mastered.) Silk was a fabric woven from the protein fibre of a silkworm, and the Chinese kept the knowledge of silk production a closely guarded secret. But that did not prevent them from showing silk off outside their empire via exports, and they often used it as a diplomatic gift. The Romans are said to have been introduced to silk somewhere in the first century BC, and just like spices, the use of which was restricted to wealthy merchants and royals, silk too was exotic and rare in Europe.[9]

The Silk Route became one of the early catalysts for other trade routes to develop, connecting the rest of Asia to Central Asia and Europe in a more fluent way. From light objects and one-offs that were transported during the early days of trade, these routes now began to facilitate large-scale transfer of a variety of products ranging from textiles, animals and animal hide to metal crafts and precious stones as well as grains, vegetables and spices. Millet, rice, pistachio, walnut, almond, apple, apricot and other stone fruit started to travel westwards or further eastwards from their places of origin in central Asia or east Asia, and gradually became common in Europe and even India.[10]

The maritime trade route that connected the west of Japan via the Indonesian spice islands and wound around India reaching the Middle East, and from there carried on to the Mediterranean region and further into Europe, came to be known as the Spice Route.

At first it may seem surprising to learn that the early travellers undertook such a treacherous journey for months at a stretch in tumultuous waters and weathers, sometimes battling pirates, to travel across the world for something as inconsequential as spices. After all, spices were not the core of one's meals, but were only used as seasoning. However, historically, spices have been given so much importance that such an arduous journey to acquire them would have seemed befitting. The course of world history across civilizations has been shaped by spices: Joseph was sold by his brothers to spice merchants as his family made its way to Egypt from Arabia; Queen Sheba gifted Solomon the spices of Arabia; and Vasco da Gama and Christopher Columbus's travelled continents in search of spices. And while in South-East Asia spices were plentiful, it took centuries before the Europeans got a whiff of that.

As more and more traders went back with stories of the spice lands in the east, spices began to be revered not only for their potent flavours but also for their medicinal and 'spiritual' properties. European and Central Asian merchants who wanted to keep the source of their spices discreet, often wove stories around spices associated with ideas of faraway exotic lands; they were mentioned in poems, and seeking them was a thing of adventure, which made them even more desirable.

Since the chilli had still not made it to India when early Europeans arrived, India's most prized spice and import back then was pepper. When the Romans gained access to the pepper that grew aplenty in the Malabar region, a new flavour was added to their otherwise wheat-, barley- and meat-based, and dominant cuisine. Like silk, ivory and pearls, pepper was sold in the Roman spice markets to wealthy businessmen.

Centuries later, in *Apicius*, a collection of Roman recipes, 349 out of the 468 recipes featured pepper as an ingredient.[11] It played such an important role in Roman kitchens and economics that Pliny the Elder, a Roman author, says,

> To think that it's only pleasing quality is pungency and that we go all the way to India to get this! Who was the first person who was willing to try it on his viands, or in his greed for an appetite was not content merely to be hungry? Both pepper and ginger grow wild in their own countries, and nevertheless they are bought by weight like gold or silver.[12]

Much later, when the English and the Dutch East India Companies vied with each other to dominate the spice trade, they ended up importing large quantities of pepper into Europe. Once the spice became affordable, it was easy to get and was used extensively in European food. Soon other spices like saffron, cumin and cloves came to be frequently added to stews, meats, pies and stuffed roasts; ginger and cinnamon went into desserts like gingerbread and tea cakes; while wines and perfumes began to be spiked with spices like cardamom, nutmeg and pepper.[13]

Unlike pepper, ginger, turmeric and cardamom were indigenously Indian; some other spices, like cinnamon, came to India via Ceylon, now Sri Lanka, and from there travelled westwards. One study indicates that cinnamon travelled with Moorish merchants to Indonesia and then to East Africa, from where it was taken to Europe by the local merchants.[14] Similarly, cloves and nutmeg were native to the Moluccas and Banda Islands (Indonesia), respectively, from where they travelled to Europe and became a part of the cuisine there. Interestingly, cinnamon is mentioned in the Old Testament (Song of Solomon), one of the oldest books, but it took decades for the Europeans to get easy access to these spices.[15]

> Your schions shall be an orchard of fruit trees, and their fruit will be pomegranates. Yours are the rarest of spices: nard and saffron, calamus and cinnamon, and all the trees that bear incense; myrrh and aloes, and all the subtlest of aromas.

The climate of India and its location on the trade routes afforded Indians a front-row view of and access to the trade of spices native to both the East and West early on in history. Especially fortunate was the country's proximity to the Malay Archipelago, or the Spice Islands (Ternate and Tidore), where clove and nutmeg grew abundantly. It is from here that these spices were brought to India, East Africa and Europe.

It wasn't just spices that crossed continental borders. The Persians and Arabs introduced greens like spinach (saag), dried fruits like almonds, cumin seeds and roses to India, among other produce. Perhaps even the okra came to India from the Middle East, making its journey from Africa (Ethiopia and Egypt),[16] though, as mentioned earlier in the book, okra may have already been available in the subcontinent since the later Indus period. Some other studies say that the *Charaka Samhita* mentioned a vegetable called bhandi/bhati, referring to it as the 'lotus of the earth'.[17]

Grapes reached China from Uzbekistan, and cinnamon and rhubarb went from the Indian subcontinent to Central Asia. Hu Sihui, a Chinese court therapist from the Yuan Dynasty founded by Ghengis Khan, is said to have developed a number of recipes inspired by India, like the ba'erbu and sasu soups, both of which used pepper (Indian) and asafoetida (Afghanistani). There is a legend that Sima Qian, a historian who reported about Chinese diplomat Zhang Qian, returned from Central Asia carrying a grapevine tendril in his rawhide sack, protecting it from the desert sun so that he could replant it.

This story reminded me of another I heard on walk in a coffee plantation in Coorg. Coffee came to India with Baba Budan, a sixth-century Sufi saint from India, who, on his journey back from the Hajj, brought back seeds of raw coffee bean from the port of Mocha in Yemen. Back then, coffee was either sold in roasted or baked form; so, no one could grow their own plantations and the monopoly on the crop rested with the Yemenis. This was until Budan managed to smuggle out seven fresh beans. He planted them in Karnataka, where coffee plantations thrived. The commercial coffee plantations of south India, though, came about much later.[18]

There is an equally interesting story about the merchant and Italian traveller Marco Polo, who travelled the Silk Route eastwards in the thirteenth century—from Venice to the Indian subcontinent via China and Ceylon. After spending some time in Sri Lanka, Polo sailed towards the Coromandel coast, and one of the things he noticed about Indians was their abstinence from animal food, which means the southern part of India may have predominantly relied on the vegetarian bounties. While passing Cape Comorin (present-day Kanyakumari) and along the coast of Malabar, he is said to have found abundant pepper and ginger, breadfruit, betel nut, palm trees and other spices.[19]

Just like Alexander's invasion of India, another important chapter in Indian history was the growth of the Mauryan empire, a time when chronology became definite for the subcontinent. The rise of this dynasty further opened mass cultural and commercial exchanges, as during this time more trade routes were established. While we have already discussed the Mauryan kitchen and how it impacted Indian cuisine in the last chapter, it is also necessary to understand their contribution to trade here.

Under Chandragupta Maurya, trade picked up rapidly. The Grand Trunk Road, popularly believed to have been built by Sher Shah Suri, and known as Sadak-e-Azam in AD 1540–1556, existed even earlier and was known as 'Uttarpatha' during the time of the Mauryan empire, from the fourth to the second century BC. It stretched from Balkh in Afghanistan to Tamralipta or Tamluk in West Bengal.[20]

Suri's Sadak stretched from Kabul in Afghanistan to Sonargaon and Bangladesh. Between the sixteenth and nineteenth centuries, the road came to be renamed as 'Badshahi Sadak' under the Mughals. The British called it the 'Long Walk' or the 'Grand Trunk Road'; from the nineteenth to the twentieth century, it ran from Kabul in Afghanistan to Chittagong in Bangladesh.

From the seventh Ashokan pillar, we come to know that in the Mauryan time, this road connected their capital of Patliputra with Taxila. Bindusara, son of Chandragupta Maurya, known as Amitrochates to the Greeks, told the Hellenistic king Antiochus, 'Send me sweet wine, dry figs and a sophist.' To which Antiochus replied, 'I hereby send you sweet wine and dry figs, but a sophist is not sold in Greece.'[21]

The Grand Trunk Road had wells at regular intervals for thirsty travellers and was lined with trees on both sides, especially mulberry bushes. Over the years, a variety of cultural and religious structures like minarets and mosques, stupas, pillars and forts came up along its sides. The road also provided for army halting points, post offices (dak), gardens, water wells (baoli) and sarais, where free food and lodging was available for travellers.[22]

This Grand Trunk Road was actually a branch of the larger Silk Route[23] that crossed India, and gradually over the years developed a unique cuisine of its own, reflecting the tastes and preferences of the travellers in each period. This cuisine included a variety of kebabs, meats cooked in tandoors, chargha (deep-fried meat), khurchan or meat scrapings, subcontinental flatbreads like the Afghani bolani,[24] bakarkhani and somle, a curd-based drink that I am tempted to think of as a predecessor of the highway lassi. (Note: curd-based drinks have existed on the Indian subcontinent since the times of the Indus Valley.) Coincidentally, the Grand Trunk Road is also where the concept of the dhaba first originated: the dusty highway was a meeting place for travellers to stop by for some grub, indulge in steamy hammams and exchange stories of adventure.

As trade flourished, the bustling Silk and Spice Routes birthed trading ports and cities such as Bukhara, Khiva, Loulan and Samarkand. The ancient routes were traversed by the Greeks, Persian kings and Mughals, and became a conduit for the exchange and development of language, lifestyle, cultural interaction and, subsequently, cuisine. And this non-tangible exchange became as important as the material exchange.

On a separate note, an ideal amalgamation of Eastern and Western cultures facilitated by these exchanges can be seen in one of the official cookbooks of the Mongol court, *Yinshan Zhengyao* (*The Proper and Essential Things for the Emperor's Food and Drink*) by Hu Sihui.[25] He was a dietary physician in the Mongol royal court, who oversaw the recipes compiled in this book for their nutritional and medicinal worth. The book was presented to Tugh Temur in 1330, and had recipes from the kitchens of Baghdad, Kashmir and eastern Europe, complete with their nutritional values as perceived by Chinese medicine of that time.[26] This was one of the first dietary manuals in Chinese history and had Mongolian, Turkic and Islamic food influences coming from the court members, who themselves had a combination of Mongol, Chinese and Central Asian origins. One of the recipes found in this book is of a roasted wolf soup flavoured with turmeric, cardamom, long pepper, pepper, saffron and vinegar.[27]

Our familiarity with many fruits, nuts and grains found in our kitchens today is in reality a result of these early exchanges. Ancient Central Asia was covered with lush forests bearing ingredients like wild pistachios, olives, cherries, walnuts, sea buckthorn, hawthorn, mountain ash and other nut-bearing trees. As agriculture took centre stage, the forests disappeared, giving way to farmlands and farmers who chose what they wanted to grow.

Irshad al-Zira'a (Guide to Agriculture), compiled in 1515 by Qasim B. Yusuf Abu Nasri Harawi, talks about cucumber, salad greens, spinach, radish, onion, garlic, beet, hemp, alfalfa, indigo, mulberry and other produce that grew abundantly in Central Asia, and many of them came to India as a result of the Persian invasion.[28]

In the previous chapters, we've already discussed how the royal Mughal kitchen affected Indian cuisine, but their influence is not just restricted there. The Mughal way of life also had an impact on trade and availability of produce in India. In Mughal texts the city of Samarkand finds special mention for the quality of its sweet fruits like apricot, melon, apple and for its grains like rice and wheat. Babur spoke about the fruits of Kabul in Afghanistan, its grapes, pomegranates, apricots, quinces, jujubes and damsons, which were found in great abundance. Samarkand and Bukhara, which were frequented by visitors from across the world, produced ingredients of the highest quality. While on the one hand Central Asia introduced the subcontinent to these items, we gave them sugar, sandalwood, coconut and spices. Abul Fazl ibn Mubarak, vizier of the Mughal emperor Akbar and author of the *Akbarnama,* whom we have met in the earlier chapters, discussed the markets of Kashmir in great detail and spoke about a thriving fruit trade.

Ever since the conquest of Kabul, Qandahar, and Kashmir, loads of fruits are imported; throughout the whole year the stores of the dealers are full, and the bazars well supplied.

Muskmelons come in season, in Hindustan, in the month of Farwardin (February–March), and are plenty in Urdibihisht (March–April). They are delicious, tender, opening, sweet smelling, especially the kinds called nashpati, babashaikhi, 'alisheri, alchah, barg-i-nai, dud-i-chiragh. They continue in season for two months longer. In the beginning of Shariwar, (August) they come from Kashmir, and before they are out of season, plenty are brought from Kabul; during the month of A'zar (November) they are imported by the caravans from Badakhshan, and continue to be had during Dai (December.) When they are in season in Zabulistan, good ones are also obtainable in the Panjab; and in Bhakkar and its vicinity they are plentiful in season, except during the forty cold days of winter. Various kinds of grapes are here to be had from Khurdad (May) to Amurdad (July), whilst the markets are stocked with Kashmir grapes during Shahnwar. Eight sers of grapes sell in Kashmir at one dam, and the cost of the transport is two rupees per man. The Kashmirians bring them on their backs in conical baskets, which look very curious. From Mihr (September) till Urdibihisht grapes come from Kabul, together with cherries, which his Majesty calls shdhalu, seedless pomegranates, apples, pears, quinces, guavas, peaches, apricots, girdalus, and aluchas, many of which fruits grow also in Hindustan. From Samarqand even they bring melons, pears, and apples.

After the Mughals, the next set of traders who impacted Indian cuisine deeply were the Portuguese. This is when Vasco da Gama comes into the picture. He arrived in Calicut (Kozhikode) in 1498 as a result of the Portuguese plunge towards the East, starting from Morocco, where they began by conquering the Madeira and Azore islands that were seeing a rapid expansion of cereal and sugarcane production. Vasco da Gama and his entourage were in search of unique produce to procure, and wanted to find new fishing grounds. At the behest of King Emmanuel of Portugal, Vasco da Gama and his troupe began their journey eastwards and eventually reached India in search of silks and spices.[29]

By then, Portugal had been trading with east and South-East Asia for centuries, and the Spice Route already linked the Indian subcontinent to the merchants and traders of the West. With so much travel happening anyway, the Portuguese realized that the Mediterranean and Arabian Seas weren't easy to navigate; it was time-consuming and there was the fear of pirates. So, they found another route, which passed through the Atlantic Sea, round the southern coast of Africa and headed towards south India. When they landed in India, the opulent lifestyle of the rajas fascinated them, persuading them to stay back much longer than they intended. While they initially came as fleeting traders, they eventually colonized the land, promoted missionary work, and married and intermingled with the locals.

As the Portuguese expanded their empire in India, their trading ports came to include Calicut on the Malabar coast, Cochin and Ceylon down south, and Chittagong in Bengal in the east. Each of these eventually became buzzing centres of trade and exchange routes between the Western world, Africa, Central Asia and India.

Throughout their time in India, the Portuguese somehow always chose to stay close to the coast, with their empire centred around Goa (whose popular city, Vasco da Gama, exists even today). They conquered the sunny state in 1510, and while initially it was just a clearing-house for the merchants from Arabia, Java, Siam, Malacca, Persia, China and even America to hop in and hop out of India, it later became the mainland for them. Many Portuguese men married Goan women, whose children ultimately became the first line of Portuguese-Indians.

Of course, the long stay of the new invaders left a mark on the history of Goan architecture, culture and cuisine, and perhaps after the Mughals, theirs is another apparent cultural imprint on India. The Portuguese ferried with them ingredients like pineapple, corn, papaya, cashew nut, sweet potato, tomato, custard apple, sapodilla and chilli, which they had gotten acquainted with during their interactions in South and Central America.[30]

Centuries before the Europeans reached South America, the Inca civilization already had a refined agricultural system that abundantly grew these ingredients as well as others like avocado, squash, beans, quinoa, yuca and tree tomatoes. But before the Portuguese, it was the Spanish travellers (Christopher Columbus and his troupe) who had discovered South and Central America through a chance encounter while attempting to find a shorter route to Asia. The Spanish in return introduced the Incas to a variety of foods like wheat, onion, lime, lemon, coconut, grapes, almond, sugar and pepper. And this is how and where Creole (mixed) cuisine originated.[31] In Mumbai, the guava is still called peru, because that is where it comes from.

Just the way chilli reached us centuries after it was first used in food preparation, Columbus brought it to Spain only in the 1400s. Portuguese traders finally introduced it across Europe and the rest of Asia (starting from the Malabar) from the fourteenth century.[32] The south Indians, who already had access to wonderful indigenous spices, welcomed the chilli into their masala box, and before one knew it the chilli became synonymous with Indian cuisine.

Apart from bringing us ingredients, the Portuguese also introduced to us certain dishes and techniques of cooking. These settlers in India had dozens of domestic helpers and cooks, mainly Goan locals, and so much culinary exchange took place between the two communities. For starters, the Portuguese were avid bakers and passed on their know-how of making culture- and starter-based breads, cakes and pastries to the Indians. In fact, even today the Goan words for bread, bread-seller and bakery come from the Portuguese words 'pão', 'poder' and 'padeiro' respectively. Though the culture of flatbread-making existed in India for centuries before this, the Portuguese taught us how to make leavened bread. This is also the reason why the word 'paowalla' is slang for Catholics even today, since it was a common profession among local Goans. Similarly, the Maharashtrian word 'batata' for potato comes from the Portuguese word for the tuber.

The Portuguese brought a variety of meat curries into Indian cuisine, like xacuti, where meat is cooked with poppy seeds and a spice paste, and cafreal. Though cafreal was originally known as piri piri, it was introduced by the Portuguese to India from their Mozambique colony. The name cafreal comes from the word 'cafre', an Islamic word for 'non-believer', also referencing the African black population. The vindaloo became an iconic dish that explains this mishmash of cultures. Its name comes from 'carne de vinha d'alhos', which is Portuguese for pork marinated in wine vinegar and garlic. Back then Indians did not have wine vinegar of their own, and so the locals fermented it using Goan palm wine and handy ingredients like tamarind, pepper, cinnamon and cardamom. Other popular dishes, like guava cheese, sorpotel, balchao, chorizo and feijoada are all Portuguese presents, as is chamuças, a variety of samosa stuffed with cardamom and cinnamon-flavoured wild meat packed in filo sheets. Besides, they also left behind surnames like D'Souza, Castro, Cruz, Dias, Fernandes, Gonsalves, Fonseca, Pereira, Rodriques, (Da) Silva, (Da) Souza and Correa, which prevail up to this day in India. The Portuguese even introduced Goan dishes like buffath, a spicy meat stew; temperado, prawns cooked in coconut milk; xacuti; and sorpotel here, as Portuguese-Indian cuisine spread through the region.

The Portuguese set up their base in Bengal in 1571, several years after their first arrival in Calicut on the west coast of India. At that time, Bengal was an independent kingdom ruled by the Muslim Lodhi dynasty, which was later taken over by the Mughals in 1576. During Emperor Akbar's reign, the Portuguese managed to acquire a village on the banks of the Hooghly (present-day Kolkata)—they had a fascination for proximity to waterbodies.[33] Their merchants were there to procure beautiful Bengali produce, like the dacca muslin (which is where the city of Dhaka gets its name from), at a cheaper price, which they then sold for a fortune in the European world, especially in Provence, Italy and Languedoc. This they did through the seventeenth century.

There is a theory that the Portuguese taught the Bengalis how to curdle milk and turn it into chenna or cheese, which forms the base of a majority of their famous sweets even today, including the rasagulla. I don't think this theory is convincing, but read on.

This theory is highly debatable because remains of pottery that were shaped in a way that allowed liquid (whey) to be strained out from milk solids were found even in the Indus Valley ruins (we have covered this in Chapter 1). Though we don't know the exact use of such vessels, some historians claim that these could have been used to make chenna or paneer, and thus these existed back then.[34] Cattle did play an important role in pre-historic Harappan and Vedic society. In fact, milk was referred to as a 'complete food'. However, we don't find the word paneer clearly mentioned until the Kushan dynasty. Literature from this period speaks of warriors consuming a solid mass of dairy made of a mixture of warm milk and curd, while the whey would be distributed among the poor.[35] The word paneer comes from the Persian, Armenian and Azerbaijani word 'panir' and the Turkish word 'peynir'—both of which refer to various preserved cheeses. However, the earliest evidence of the word's usage can be found among the Bakhtiari, a nomadic Iranian tribe from the Isfahan region, who developed a cheese called 'paneer-khiki', which literally translates to 'container and skin'.[36] This made sense to me, as the Kushan empire did stretch from India towards central Asia and the Middle East. And that's why I wouldn't give credit to the Portuguese for paneer.

However, they can be credited for introducing cheeses like the Bandel—invented in Bandel in West Bengal—to India. Before these cheeses, we had little acquaintance with any cheese indigenous to India. Originally, a typical Bengali meal would consist of simple Indian staples like rice, leafy vegetables, gourd, eggplant, fish, fruits like banana, mango, coconut and pomegranate; there was also a rich intake of milk and ghee. But with trade routes opening up and merchants going in and out of Bengal, there was an advent of newer ingredients, like oranges, litchis and pears imported from China, spices like cinnamon, cardamom and clove, which became abundantly available from other spice regions, and also potato, tomato and chilli.

In general, Calcutta experienced cultural diversity like no other place in India. Apart from Portugal, cross-cultural influences came from Armenia too. In the nineteenth century, Bengal was experiencing an industrial revolution and saw an influx of mining communities from Armenia, who settled here. (This was not the first time Armenians had settled in India—one of Akbar's queens was Armenian, as well as his chief justice and some influential merchants, and there were Armenian settlements in Delhi, Agra, Lahore and the port of Surat.[37]) When the British came, they had established trade with the Armenians by accepting funding from them to buy land in Bengal. Armenians did impact Indian cuisine, although not too deeply. For example, a parallel can be found between the Bengali and Armenian dolmas: both are stuffed preparations,[38] one of vegetables stuffed with rice and meats, while the other is meat stuffed in vine leaves. [39]

Then, around the 1800s, there was a movement of immigrants from Baghdad to Bombay and Calcutta, who brought in their own culinary techniques and adapted their cuisine to the flavours of their new land. These were the Jews, who so far had had minimal access to spices. Sure, they had previously cooked with garlic and chilli, but it was here that ingredients like ginger and turmeric were added to their cuisine. These additions and adaptations gave rise to a whole new hybrid Jewish cuisine, which had preparations like arook (meaning veined, in Hebrew and Arabic), rice balls flavoured with garam masala; pantras, beef-stuffed pancakes sprinkled with turmeric, ginger and garam masala; hanse mukhmura, a duck-based dish where the meat is cooked with almonds, raisins, bay leaf, tamarind paste and ginger root; and aloo-m-kalla murgi, pot-roasted chicken with potatoes. [40]

Kolkata also birthed the famous Indo-Chinese cuisine around the late nineteenth and early twentieth centuries. Chinese immigrants, known as Hakkas—which literally translates to 'guest family'—were locally also referred to as nomads or gypsies. They began to settle in large numbers in Madras and southern Calcutta, and this Hakka-speaking group mainly worked in tanneries, at ports, as shoemakers, carpenters, dentists and later in beauty salons. They predominantly settled in an area called Tangra in Kolkata. This was also the first and only Chinatown in an Indian city.

The Tangras got with them their methods of cooking Chinese food, but the availability of new ingredients led to an entirely new kind of cuisine, known as Tangra cuisine or Chindian. With an array of Indian spices now available to them, the Hakkas experimented by adapting to local flavours. They adapted and used chicken instead of just beef and pork, added hot spice pastes made of green and red chillies to their food, flavoured it abundantly with ginger, garlic, coriander and in some cases even kashundi (Bengali mustard paste) and cumin. The cuisine led to some innovative and bizarre dishes, like egg-drop soup, thread chicken or bhetki (deep-fried like a pakora), dragon chicken, chow mein, gold coin prawns, drums of heaven and other things that purist Chinese-food enthusiasts would certainly not recognize.[41]

The cuisine trickled to other parts of the country too. In Delhi, it became Chinjabi (a mixture of Chinese and, mind you, Punjabi cuisine). I will tell you my personal story about Chinese food in Mumbai. I have not only eaten Tangra-style spicy chilli and garlic noodles and fried rice served in red plastic plates at nooks and crannies of Mumbai's khau gullies (eating lanes). I have also had this crazy-delicious version of Chinese food at the umpteen parties I attended, where the food was cooked by 'Chinese maharajas'. In a Gujarati home, the term 'maharaj' usually refers to a cook. Those who specialized in Indian-Chinese were called 'dhapas', which I later find out, comes from an area in Tangra in Kolkata called Dhapa.

This leads me to reiterate the fact that throughout Indian history, travellers continued pouring into India. After the

Portuguese, the Dutch East India Company (Verenigde Oost-Indische Compagnie) was established in 1602. Though the Dutch left fewer imprints on our cuisine and culture, their entry was important, setting the base for the East Indian empire, which was strengthened in the seventeenth century and further stirred the making of Indian cuisine. The capital city of the Dutch East India Company was Batavia (present-day Jakarta in Indonesia) and their main trading centres were Pulicat in Tamil Nadu, Chinsurah, near Hooghly in Bengal, and Surat in India.

The Dutch wanted to monopolize the spice market and get rid of competitors like the Portuguese, English and Asian merchants. During this time, spices were still bartered for a variety of goods like cloth, sugar, gold and other spices. The Dutch, with the hope of monopolizing the spice trade, signed agreements with the spice islands to supply ingredients like nutmeg, mace and cloves exclusively to them; but the Indian pepper, which was of utmost importance, could not be monopolized.[42]

Though Dutch cuisine and food habits didn't percolate deeply into India or Indonesia, their own cuisine was influenced by these new-found ingredients. They traded heavily in pepper, cinnamon, cloves, tea, rice, coffee, nutmeg and mace from the Indian subcontinent, and so added these to their own kitchens. Even today, some of their popular dishes are laced with spices that they may have been familiarized with during their long stay in the Indian subcontinent. It is ritualistic for them to scrape nutmeg on top of their vegetables before they begin eating them, and there is a phrase for it—'en beetje nootmuskaat' or 'and a little nutmeg'.[43] Besides, every kitchen will have a handy nutmeg grater. Their cheeses too are studded with clove and cumin, and a few of their popular desserts—like speculoos cookies, kruidnoten, pepernoten, jan hagel, stroopwafels and taai-taai—all contain powdered spices.

The Dutch set up a few of the subcontinent's early coffee plantations in Java, Indonesia (one of the colonies they traded with the British for India). By the mid-1600s, when coffee was becoming popular in New Amsterdam (a Dutch settlement in South Manhattan) as a popular European drink, it was also gaining popularity in India.[44]

Much later, but still because of the Europeans, chai made an entry in India. No, the Mughals didn't get to sip on masala chai in their rose gardens, and you and I would not wake up to its grassy, milky aroma had it not been for this brand of traders.

Albert de Mandelslo, a German traveller who visited the port of Surat in 1638, is recorded to have said:

> At our ordinary meeting every day we took only the, which is commonly used all over the Indes, not only among those of the country, but also among the Dutch and the English, who take it as a drug that cleanses the stomach, and digests the superfluous humours, by a temperate heat particular thereto.

A chaplain from Surat, the Reverend John Ovington, in his book *Voyage to Surat* in the year 1689, says, 'Tea likewise is a common Drink with all the Inhabitants of *India*, as well *Europeans* as Natives; and by the *Dutch* is used as such a standing Entertainment, that the Tea-pot's seldom off the Fire, or unemploy'd.' He also mentions how the baniya community (the Indian traders) excessively drank tea, mixing it with some spices and hot water, and how some Indians consumed it with sugar candy or lemon.[45]

We will talk about tea later in this chapter.

After the Dutch came the French, who too expanded their overseas endeavours around the 1600s. By then, Spain, Portugal, Britain and Holland were already setting up colonies around the world, especially here in the East. The French not only had aspirations for trade, they were also here to spread their religion, their language and culture, and were looking for fresh land to cultivate tobacco, wheat and sugar, which were fetching good rates in the European market. By now their own kitchens had adopted the potato, tomato, maize, clove, nutmeg, pepper and other spices, which they didn't have frequent access to before the trade routes opened up.

In India, they set up their base in Pondicherry, Karaikal and Yanaon on the Coromandel Coast, Mahe on the Malabar Coast and Chandernagore in West Bengal. Unlike the Portuguese or the British, but like the Dutch, the French didn't influence our cuisine too much, and there are barely any traces of French impact in Indian cooking, or vice versa.

One of the reasons could be that French chefs would not entertain adaptations and changes in cuisine. They also had their notions of culinary supremacy. Although the biggest takeaway for most Europeans from India were the spices, the French may have felt that too many spices took away or disguised flavours rather than enhanced them.

Traces of French colonization can still be seen in areas like Chandernagore, where until the 1960s schools taught French cuisines people spoke the language. The Bengali and the French also share a commonality of eating meals course by course, and modern cafes in Pondicherry serve French-influenced food like salad Niçoise, crepes, ratatouille, coq au vin and bouillabaisse even today.

Finally, the most important chapter of India's cultural, political and culinary history began with the advent of the British. They were in constant battle with the French to gain more of Indian land, and some colonies like Coromandel kept changing hands between the two. Just like the other colonizers, the British too came to India to trade in the seventeenth century and ended up conquering the land, seeing its tremendous monetary and political potential.

Spices aside, the other Indian item that attracted them was opium. Back then, Bengal produced large quantities of opium, which had a massive market in China, and the British would supply shiploads of it to the southern Chinese ports through Hooghly, across the Bay of Bengal, the Malacca Strait and the South China Sea. The Chinese sent the ships back with tea. Thus, poppy and tea became available aplenty in India. This also explains the ample use of the seeds of opium (poppy) in Bengali cuisine, known as posto.

This brings me to chai, the most popular Indian drink. India is today one of the world's largest producers of tea, with over 13,000 gardens and a workforce of more than two million involved in its production. A certain kind of wild tea plant is said to have existed in the north-eastern part of the Indian subcontinent, Burma, Thailand, the Himalayan belt and Tibet.[46] To speak of commercial tea, the Dutch first brought tea seeds from China in the seventeenth century, and it was the British who were responsible for its domestication and its popularity here. It is important to note that the later Mughals too enjoyed tea, which was mainly supplied from China. But only when the British set up their own tea plantations did it gave birth to Indian tea. The plantations came up across the country, in areas like Assam, the Himalayan foothills, including the Kumaon region, Dehradun, Garhwal, the Kangra valley, Kulu, and even as far as Darjeeling.

But tea still hadn't become the masala chai as we know it. This boiled-with-ample-milk-and-sugar version, the shade of Huda Teddy lipstick, only came in years later. Drinking tea with sugar was certainly not an Asian habit, and one doesn't know when the English began drinking their sweetened tea. However, we know that when the British ladies hosted afternoon tea parties, sugar bowls, tongs and silver spoons were laid out to make the beverage, and it was fashionable for the British women to keep these accessories in their closets. Tea was often savoured with sweet ginger biscuits or sugary cakes.

Though spices brought the Europeans to India and textiles kept them here, it was tea's popularity that eventually took over textiles for the East India Company between 1700 and 1774, as it became the most valuable trading commodity.[47] After setting up plantations and exporting tea, the British-led tea associations wanted tea to become popular for the Indians too. Fortunately for them, it became an emotion.

Tea promotion began with the setting up of stalls in factories, mines and mills, and workers were allowed tea breaks to grab the drink. In the trains of the Indian Railways, men were hired and placed strategically at stations with kettles and 'cutting-chai' glasses.[48] The chaiwalas across the country clinked through the night and early hours of dawn with the rhythmic 'chai, chai, chai', which probably rings in your ears even today every time you think of journeying by passenger train.

Similarly, they also introduced us to the concept of biscuits. In fact, the Hindu Biscuit Company, which later came to be known as Britannia, was created to meet their biscuit needs in India. A side story is that much later, when the Swadeshi movement was gaining momentum, Parle-G, one of India's most iconic biscuits, was established to counter the popularity of British-led brands like Britannia, United Biscuits, Huntley & Palmers and Glaxo. But more on that in the next chapter.

The British didn't meddle with the core ideas of Indian cuisine, like our style of eating a dal, chawal, subji, salad and roti as a meal. But they picked up a lot of nuances and incorporated them into their meal habits.

As they found firmer footing here, they had to tweak their diets, keeping in mind the difference in weather conditions here from what it was back home. Heavy meat roasts, puddings and casseroles gave way to the idea of a light luncheon, and with this came the idea of 'tiffin'. The meaning ascribed to this word is not straightforward. It derives from the English slang 'tiffing', which means to take a little drink, and this word itself comes from the word 'tiff', which was a popular diluted liquor back then. Since they ate a light lunch mid-afternoon, at 2–3 p.m., probably with a quick sip of this liquor, the meal came to be known as a 'tiffin'.

Their style of lunch boxes, quite popular across the West, consisted of stacked tins. Originally designed by R.J. Reynolds in Wisconsin, who was inspired by the reuse of tobacco and cookie tins by miners to pack their lunch, this multi-layered lunch box eventually became iconic to Indian cuisine and design aesthetic. For the British, their tiffins included curries, kebabs and leftover meats, which they packed to work the next day with some added fresh spices. This method may have given rise to a popular Indian dish called jalfrezi, which is technically a distinct way of using up leftover meat.

The British introduced us to beers, clubhouses and the concept of the gymkhana, which literally stood for 'gym' or gymnasiums and 'khana' or food. Sometimes the memsahibs met here over cups of tea and the boys played cricket. They also developed a drink called the punch. Derived from the Hindi word 'paanch', which means five, the original punch was a combination of a native Indian brew mixed with sugar, spices or tea, water and lime juice. It became a staple at the white sahib's parties, and the sailors and employees of the British East India Company who went back to England took it with them. From there it spread across Europe and to America.[49]

The memsahibs with their Indian cooks developed unique dishes with strong European roots, but peppered (pun intended) with Indian masalas. Some of these were the mulligatawny soup, dak bungalow chicken, Bengal lancer's shrimp curry, bad-word curry, railway lamb, kedgeree and country captain chicken. These contained influences from the kitchens of both cultures. The emergence of Anglo-Indian food is by far the most distinct example of how colonization resulted in the development of a whole new cuisine.

The term Anglo-Indian referred to Brit-Indians, and is also colloquially applied to children of Indians who married other Europeans who came before the British. For example, when the Portuguese were here, one of their governors, Afonso De Albuquerque, encouraged marriage between Portuguese men and Indian women of the rich classes as a way to spread Christianity. Their children were known as Luso-Indians, or the first Eurasians. Similarly, the Dutch intermingled with the locals in the Malabar and Coromandel coasts and in Bengal, marrying their women. Dutch surnames are evident even today in the towns of Negapatam (today's Nagapattinam), Chinsurah and Pulicat. Similarly, the French intermarried with local Indians in Pondicherry and Chandernagore. The common denominator was that Anglo-Indians had at least one Indian parent, mostly the mother, and a European father.[50]

Over time, Anglo-Indians developed a unique culture of their own, and a cuisine that wasn't similar to that of other Indians. Their households had at least three or four Indian helps, including a sweeper, a gardener, a washerman and a khansamah who took care of the kitchen. The ideal pantry was filled with rice, lentils, flours and Indian vegetables and meats, but also stocked ample supplies of tinned provisions like English bacon, Danish butter, Australian jams, Kraft cheese, pickles, chutneys, homemade preserves and homemade carrot wine.[51]

They liberally used Indian ingredients, depending on which part of the country they were settled in, so you'll find coconut and spices being used down south and curd being used in the north. Those in Maharashtra or Goa ate cabbage or red pumpkin foogath, beef or mutton buffath, chicken shakuti, pickled pork vindaloo and amti. Dishes like chops and cutlets made of minced meat, fish, egg or vegetables, shaped in oval moulds, became a Bengali staple. Anglo-Indians still cooked their roasts, stews and pies, but ate curries, kebabs, koftas and pulaos too. Festivities called for special feasts in the Anglo-Indian home, and were marked not only by specialities like rich plum cake, coconut pie, custard, trifle, pudding soaked in rum, chocolate fudge and rum punch, but also gulab jamun, vermicelli, firni, and sweets like the dodol, marzipan and kul kul.

And while the British were the last of the prominent outside influences to impact Indian cuisine, I would say it was essentially the arrival of the Persians and the Portuguese that led to all the major changes in Indian cuisine. It was they who lifted Indian cuisine from a basic millet, vegetable, curry and rice portfolio to include a variety of gravies, flatbreads, pulaos, kebabs, refined sweet dishes, cheeses and introduced newer fruits, vegetables and spices that the land did not have earlier.

5

CONCLUSION

This brings me to the last chapter of this book. Even though the British stayed in India for over 200 years and were the last of the many external influences, there are not many tangible changes, recipes or additions that they weaved into Indian cuisine. This is especially true if you compare them with influences coming from the Central Asians or the Portuguese. Having said that, Indian royals who mingled with them, picked up their habits, pantry staples, culinary etiquette, choice of crockery, eating style and so on.

Post their departure, Indian food went through several organic changes of its own, owing to the partition of the country, influences from political figures of independent India, the impact of modernization, access to newer ingredients and the privatization of media and that is what we will explore in this concluding note.

For me, one of the characters in Indian history who had a whimsical relationship with food is the poet Rabindranath Tagore. Like all the finer things in life such as art and literature that he indulged in, Tagore's food choices were refined and almost like poetry themselves. One of his early works reads:

Aamshotto dudhey pheli, tahatey kodoli doli,
Shondesh makhia dia tatey
Hapush-hupush shobdo, charidik nistobdho,
Pipira kandia jae paate.

(Aamshotto or sun-dried ripe mango mixed in milk, along with banana and shondesh (sweet). The sound of slurping echoes in the silence, making even ants [pipira] return, shedding tears into the empty plate because there's nothing left for them.)[1]

The Bengali bard had a playful relationship with food throughout his life, like a certain other national leader, but I will come to the second person later. At Tagore's Khamkheyali Sabha (Assembly of the Whimsical)—an informal club where his friends and he would feast on dishes and exchange dialogue—he insisted that only unique food should be served. The Tagores had a habit of collecting menus from across their travels, and then replicating some of them in the kitchen at Jorasanko Thakur Bari, their ancestral home. No one visiting them would be sent back on an empty stomach; though Rabindranath himself was a sparse eater, he insisted on sharing food with everyone around.

Like a modern-day restaurant, Tagore's kitchen was cuisine-agnostic; so, they made everything from a British pie and a Turkish kebab to Bengali gravies and food from different parts of India. He personally loved bhapa ilish (steamed hilsa), roasted mutton cooked with pineapple and European food like cream of tomato soup or salmon in Hollandaise sauce.[2]

His curious demands were often executed by his wife Mirnalini, and out of such experiments, Tagore cuisine was born. It features dishes like jackfruit yoghurt 'fish' curry (which had no fish), mutton in mustard paste, parwal and prawn raita, jimikand jalebi, dahi malpua and other extremely bizarre combinations.[3] For me, the kabishambardhana barfi takes the cake (quite literally). The recipe has been under wraps for decades even though it was invented in his kitchen by his niece for his fiftieth birthday. If you thought cauliflower pizza was bizarre, hear this: this phoolkopir barfi is made of boiled cauliflower florets mixed with sugar and khoya!

Tagore was nothing short of a top food influencer of his time. He was such a vision that he featured in advertizing campaigns for brands such as Cadbury's Bournvita and Godrej's vegetable soap. He also wrote a short poem dedicated to tea lovers waiting for the water to boil for Lipton Tea. He himself drank Sanatogen, a then-popular health supplement powder, and sometimes even Chinese jasmine or chrysanthemum tea. Though he was predominantly a meat eater, in 1894, after chancing upon a domestic fowl grappling for life, he gave up animal meat and turned vegetarian.

This brings me to the second figure—Mahatma Gandhi—whose pro-vegetarian ideology continues to shape the entire nation's emotions towards meat-eating even today. Like Tagore, Gandhi too had an experimental relationship with food. Firstly, he led a national movement on the back of a common kitchen ingredient, salt: the Salt Satyagraha of 1930. A civil disobedience movement, it protested the British-levied salt tax, and Gandhi said he chose salt because an item of daily use would resonate more with all classes of citizens than an abstract demand for greater political rights.[4] More about his dietary preferences can be found in *An Autobiography or the Story of My Experiments with Truth*. In one of the chapters, Gandhi talks extensively about converting to vegetarianism. In his youth, he was a committee member of the Vegetarian Society in England; that is where he discovered the pillars of vegetarianism and began his own experiments with a plant-based diet.

He recollects giving up on Indian sweets and condiments too at one point, and says that the real seat of taste was not the tongue but the mind. Gandhi assessed many diets and ultimately settled for one that is freakishly similar to mine!

He mentions one of his 11-day experiments in the summer of 1893, when he ate nothing but raw food.[5] During the Salt Satyagraha, he remained a staunch advocate of a salt-free diet, giving up on salt in his food for years. He went off tea, coffee, chocolate and even eggs. In the book he says,

There were many minor experiments going on along with the main one; as for example, giving up starchy foods at one time, living on bread and fruit alone at another, and once living on cheese, milk, and eggs. This last experiment is worth noting. It lasted not even a fortnight. The reformer who advocated starchless food had spoken highly of eggs, and held that eggs were not meat. It was apparent that there was no injury done to living creatures in taking eggs. I was taken in by this plea, and took eggs in spite of my vow. But the lapse was momentary. I had no business to put a new interpretation on the vow. The interpretation of my mother who administered the vow was there for me. I knew that her definition of meat included eggs. And as soon as I saw the true import of the vow I gave up eggs and the experiment alike.

This meant that unless I knew what was what, I had to go through the awkward process of ascertaining whether a particular course contained eggs or no, for many puddings and cakes were not free from them. But though the revelation of my duty caused this difficulty, it simplified my food. The simplification in its turn brought me annoyance, in that I had to give up several dishes I had come to relish. These difficulties were only passing, for the strict observance of the vow produced an inward relish distinctly more healthy, delicate, and permanent.[6]

His food choices were not just dietary but also made a political statement. For example, going off sugar and chocolate were linked to protesting the exploitation of slave labour and the imperialism on plantations across the world,[7] although there is a famous story of him quitting sugar to set an example for a young man with a sugar addiction. To put Gandhi's diet in a nutshell, he was almost vegan (didn't consume cow's milk), ate raw food, switched between various kinds of diets, avoided processed food and fasted. If the publishers allowed a woke millennial meme, I would add it here!

Similarly, other political figures from the twentieth century had peculiar preferences. For example, Jawaharlal Nehru had a weak spot for tandoori chicken, especially from Delhi's Moti Mahal. Apparently, it even featured often on his official banquet menus. Nehru famously allotted a plot to the owners Kundan Lal Gujral, Kundan Lal Jaggi and Thakur Dass to help them expand their business. I have more to share on Gujral's story, but we will come to that later.

National leaders aside, Indian cuisine was affected severely by political changes, especially the Partition in 1947. When India was divided into two separate nations, it changed the geography of the region and, as a consequence, its cuisine. Millions fled/moved between India and the newly formed Pakistan. Delhi particularly attracted a large number of refugees as it was an obvious choice for those looking for lucrative economic opportunities. With this migration, culture and cuisine also shifted. As refugees longed for food from their land, a sudden influx of Punjabi eateries could be seen in the capital. In her book *Mrs LC's Table*, my friend Anoothi Vishal writes,

What the city lost in terms of its artful, elaborate dishes was replaced by newer, bolder, tomato-laden flavours from western Punjab. As a new immigrant community poured in from across the border, new tastes and techniques gained ground. Tandoori became the food of Delhi. Mughlai, the older cuisine that had come about as a result of a composite culture of Shahjahanabad, has faded.[8]

One such immigrant was Kundan Lal, founder of Moti Mahal, the reason why tandoori chicken got introduced to Indian cuisine. Gujral previously ran a dhaba at Gora Bazar in Peshawar, where he served dishes like kebabs, dal, kormas, roti, naan, paranthas, kulfis and fruit cream. He brought some of these, including the tandoori chicken, to India and left a historic mark on Indian cuisine. The story goes that the popularity of tandoori chicken often led to a surplus of meat pieces; when Lal didn't know what to do with them, he added them to a tomato-butter-cream gravy and thus was born butter chicken. Other additions to Delhi's repertoire included Multani moth kachori: a moth bean gravy topping crispy broken kachoris, dahi bhalle, papri chaat and dal makhani. The same period also introduced Delhi to 'Punjabi' dishes like paneer-laden gravies, rajma–chawal, chole, shahi paneer, kadai paneer and other dishes that even today are sold under the term 'Mughalai cuisine'.[9] The refined Mughal yoghurt-based gravies made way for a tomato-and-chilli base, changing the face of Delhi's food forever. Consequently, restaurants that previously catered to the British and sold cutlets, puddings and pies were now catering to Punjabi families and so tweaked their menus too. The Hindu-Sindhis from Sindh, in present-day Pakistan, brought with them the Sindhi papad and pickle culture.

In a similar manner, the partition of Bengal into West Bengal and East Bengal led to another round of changes. There was a steady migration from present-day Bangladesh to Kolkata in 1947 (it further increased in 1971, post Bangladesh's war of independence). The migrants (known as Bangals), longed for food from their homeland (East Bengal) and that changed the food culture of Kolkata just like Delhi. Ghotis, inhabitants of West Bengal, got access to countryside Bengali greens such as notay saag, paat saag, kochu sak and shapla, which were not as widely available in the city back then. Due to its high demand, such ingredients started being sold in temporary markets, and later in mainstream markets, set up in the city to meet the needs of these new residents. Originally, West Bengal had a rich Vaishnav influence, with food that did not make heavy use of garlic and onion. But post Partition, there was a heavy demand for these greens and also varieties of fish like amodi, loitta, chitol and aar, and Kolkata's shutki maach (dried fish) business shot up thanks to the Bangals because Ghotis didn't eat much dry fish before. Even today, many of these items, such as saags and aar, are eaten mainly by East Bengalis. Sweets such as chamcham and bhapa doi that famously originated in East Bengal became popular here[10]—especially a sweet called khaja, which is available only in a handful of sweet shops in present-day Kolkata.

There were also other smaller changes like in 1971, when Turtuk, one of the gateways to the Siachen Glacier, became a part of India—it was under Pakistani control until the Indian Army captured the village. A new cuisine, known as Balti, became as much a part of Indian cuisine as any other like Gujarati or Malayali. Bearing influences from the cuisines of Baltistan, Pakistan, Afghanistan and India, Baltistani food still remains untapped. What is popularly known as Balti food in the UK is actually British-Balti cuisine and has little or zero semblance with food that is originally from this region. The British version includes spicy curries served in metal kadhais (in Hindi balti means a bucket) in curry houses run by South Asian immigrants. But real Balti food is so rare, it can seldom be found outside certain pockets of Ladakh or even on Google for that matter. Dishes like kisir, buckwheat pancake; tsamik, a yoghurt- and herb-based dip; fay mar, roasted barley flour mixed with white butter; ba-leh, local hand-rolled noodles; grangthur, fluffy buckwheat bread; chonmagramgrim, a salad of tomato, apple, walnut, apricots and yak cheese salad; and phading, a dessert of boiled apricots, are some of the dishes from this area.

While political movements have affected Indian cuisine throughout history, there were some profound changes in food availability and dissemination of resources post-Independence. One of the main priorities of the new government was to generate food security. So, in 1965, the Green Revolution was rolled out with the help of geneticist and administrator M.S. Swaminathan. His aim was for Indian farms to grow more high-yielding varieties (HYV) of crops, expand farmlands, practice double cropping, mechanize agriculture, promote the usage of fertilizers and pesticides, and encourage the usage of irrigation. As a result of this modernization, India's agricultural production was definitely boosted, but our indigenous crops and eating habits became a casualty of that development. The farmers shifted focus from native varieties of rice, millets and lentils that they previously grew to hybrid crops that would flourish easily and in large quantities. The Green Revolution strengthened India's food security but subsequently led to the extinction of several crops and therefore we left behind an important slice of our culinary life. As farmers moved to grow new HYV of rice, wheat and soybean, we lost almost one lakh varieties of indigenous rice and several varieties of millets, lentils, barley and groundnuts.[11] Most importantly, we moved from being a millet-eating nation to a rice-eating one.

In 1970, the White Revolution or Operation Flood was launched. It was kick-started by Dr Verghese Kurien, a boy from Kerala who later went on to become the chairman of Amul, India's largest dairy cooperative society. Kurein created a national milk grid, linking milk producers throughout the country. The board, which helped in controlling seasonal price fluctuations, generated income in rural India and ensured that milk producers got a major share of the income from their end consumers. Thanks to this, India became a self-dependent nation in milk production and is now the world's largest producer of milk, with 22 per cent of global production. But that too came with its set of drawbacks, like a loss of indigenous cattle and farmers converting forest land into grazing grounds.

Post modernization, several food companies boomed in India. Amul is one such example. But way before Amul, one of India's oldest food companies was set up by Vadilal Gandhi. He started off as a soda shop owner in Ahmedabad in 1907, making ice cream using a traditional kothi method, where a hand-operated machine that used ice and salt churned the milk. In 1926, his son Ranchod Lal opened a small retail outlet and eventually passed the business to his sons Ramchandra and Lakshman, who expanded it further.[12] In 1950, the popularity of Vadilal (the brand) grew when it introduced an Indian variant of the popular Italian cassata cake as an ice cream. The rainbow-hued dessert became synonymous with Vadilal and can be credited to being India's first gourmet ice cream experience. By the late 1970s, Kwality, Joy and Vadilal had major shares in the ice cream industry in India. At this time, Vadilal's monopoly in vegetarian ice creams is what helped it remain ahead of the curve.

Another popular food brand that put India on the global map was Parle. It launched in 1929, and in 1947, when India became independent, the company launched an ad campaign showcasing its Glucose biscuits as an Indian alternative to British biscuits. Parle gave India one of the most iconic products that has world recognition today, the Parle-G biscuit. As of 2020, as per Nielsen, Parle-G is the largest selling biscuit brand in the world, beating Kraft's Oreo, Wal-Mart's private labels and Mexico's Gamesa.[13]

The food industry flourished and so did restaurants. In the 1900s, Gaylord opened in Mumbai's posh Marine Drive by

Pishori Lal Lamba, a Delhi-based restaurateur, and Iqbal Ghai. They had previously founded the Kwality Group, a hospitality brand that launched the Kwality Restaurant in Delhi in 1947. While some restaurants like Leopold's Cafe and Bademiyan in Mumbai, Indian Coffee House in Kolkata, Dorabjee and Sons in Pune existed since the 1800s, the 1900s saw more shops like Tunday Kababi in Lucknow, Kesar Da Dhaba in Amritsar, Britannia and Co in Mumbai, Mavalli Tiffin Room in Bengaluru, Glenary's in Darjeeling, Karim's and United Coffee House in Delhi and Flury's in Kolkata open, catering to this New India. Many of these food establishments have gained an iconic status and are busy even today, serving dishes that are a hundred years old.

I even found a treasure of post-Independence cuisine in vintage Indian cookbooks, while in Chapter 3, I have spoken about *Ni'matnama*, a collection of recipes from the Malwa Sultanate, *Alwan-e-Nemat* from Jahangir's period and *Nuskha-e-Shahjahani*, which had Shah Jahan's recipes. In the nineteenth and twentieth centuries, some cookbooks, like *Culinary Jottings for Madras* and *The Indian Cookery Book: A Practical Handbook to the Kitchen in India* came out. The former was written by a colonel in the Indian Army, who was a resident of Madras and spent his time writing about food in the local newspapers. Apart from recipes, the book also had a set of instructions for the memsahibs that included how to cope with Indian kitchen staff, party menus, stocking the pantry and how to cook Western food using local ingredients. His knowledge of Anglo-Indian cookery and Victorian haute cuisine became so popular that when he went back to Britain, he set up a successful cookery school in London.

Then there were several early Indian cookbooks written by some of the most iconic writers from different communities of India. Most were written by women and so were ahead of their time. Take for instance *Pakwan Pothi* and *Pakwan Sagar*, two of the earliest Indian cookbooks featuring Parsi recipes, followed by *Vividh Vani* (1894), a two-volume cookbook written by Meherbai Jamsetjee Wahadia, featuring recipes like akuri and patiyo besides English staples like puddings and tarts. *Vividh Vani* was the first Gujarati cookbook to be written by a woman. There were others like S. Meenakshi Ammal's *Samaithu Paar* (1961), a Tamil cuisine cookbook, Kamalabai Ogale's *Ruchira* (1970), a guide to Marathi cooking, B.F. Varghese's *Recipes for All Occasions* (1974), a mandatory cookbook for Keralan households, and my personal favourite, *The Pleasures of Vegetarian Cooking* by Tarla Dalal (1974). Some of these books are in print even today and were not only an important part of every Indian woman's bookshelves back then, but also carry-alongs as a part of their daughter's wedding trousseau.

What connects them is that all were written by women and not only featured Indian recipes but some also introduced housewives to the world of international flavours. For example, Varghese's cookbook displays her Syrian Christian heritage alongside diverse international flavours like Armenian kebabs. Dalal's book is known to teach women how to make traditional food, but also Tex-Mex and Italian, among other cuisines. Most of these recipe books are further populated with ideas on hosting great parties, setting the right menu, buying ingredients and stocking the pantry, and other ways of managing the kitchen.

Apart from books, television influenced the way we ate. Post liberalization, India experienced a change in media ownership, and so the monopoly of broadcasting shifted from the government to private players. It was only in 1992 that Zee TV, India's first private entertainment channel launched in Hindi. While earlier the programming focused on informational and developmental content, now the emphasis shifted to educational and instructional material. In their second year, Zee TV launched India's first cookery show *Khana Khazana*, with chef Sanjeev Kapoor as the face of the programme. Every Sunday morning, families sat together to watch a happy Punjabi boy cook dishes that hit a sweet spot between achievable and aspirational. I remember my sister meticulously jotting down his vegetarian recipes in her 'Khana Khazana notebook'. Kapoor wasn't just a good-looking chef; his early recipes like navratan korma, masala dosa, dahi bhalle, lentil soup and barbecue prawns were spot-on and they helped Indians cook 'restaurant-like' food at home. The show ran for over 600 episodes and Kapoor's signature smile was as consistent as his dialogue 'namak swada anusar'. The then executive chef of Centaur Hotel in Juhu, Mumbai, he went on to become one of India's most iconic chefs. While several other chefs auditioned for this role, it was Chef Kapoor who stood out for his ability to teach home chefs what they would be able to cook versus displaying superior cooking skills.

In the UK, Madhur Jaffrey was already hosting cooking shows for the BBC at least a decade before Kapoor. Her first show *Madhur Jaffrey's Indian Cookery* dropped in 1982, followed by *Far Eastern Cookery* and *Flavours of India*. Why is her story important? Because unlike the USA, the UK's food scene was greatly influenced by Indian cuisine and we will talk more about that soon. Jaffrey was a multi-hyphenate who presented on radio, was an alumnus of the Royal Academy of Dramatic Art in England and acted in several plays and movies. Mainly, she wrote over thirty cookbooks dedicated to Indian cuisine and helped set the tone for how Indian food was going to be perceived internationally for decades to come.

Her shows tried to present Indian cuisine to the British as something beyond the curries that they were familiar with. Sure, she indulged them with chicken tikka, vindaloo and rogan josh, but also raan masaldar and erachi ularthiyathu, dishes that were not as widely spoken about back then. She became one of the foremost female ambassadors of Indian cuisine.

I also want to add that Londoners had access to Indian cuisine as early as 1810, with the first official Indian food restaurant, Hindoostane Coffee House, opening in Portman Square, Mayfair. It was owned by Sake Dean Mohammed, a Bengali surgeon from the British East India Company, and served versions of what may be called 'Indian' food back then. Curry houses had been booming in Britain since the eighteenth century as the East India Company's men travelled from the Indian subcontinent and missed home food, and this fascination only grew with curry-rice specialty restaurants opening in various areas around London, including Piccadilly.[14] However, this was not real Indian food, and diners often had to choose from the most cliched items such as jalfrezi, Madras curry, vindaloo, rogan josh, korma, dopiaza, gobi aloo, naan and tadka dal. Most curries were dished out in the unsightly baltis I spoke about earlier in this chapter, thereby giving birth to British-Balti cuisine. Even today, if you look up ready-made Indian sauces on global grocery websites, these are still the first few options to show up. The old Indian restaurants of London were mainly run by Bangaldeshis and Pakistanis serving a version of Indian subcontinental food.

In 1926, Edward Palmer, the great-grandson of an English general and an Indian-Mughal princess, opened Veeraswamy in Piccadilly. The restaurant broke new ground and happens to be London's oldest surviving Indian restaurant. These days, the menu features chicken makhani, rogan josh and pineapple curry, but back when it opened, it was an it-spot for the rich and the famous to hang out. Veeraswamy changed the UK's perception of Indian food from being a cheap eat to being fashionable.

The UK's fascination with Indian food became more apparent in 2001, when Britain's then foreign minister Robin Cook declared chicken tikka masala as their national dish. In his speech he said:

> Chicken Tikka Masala is now a true British national dish, not only because it is the most popular, but because

it is a perfect illustration of the way Britain absorbs and adapts external influences. Chicken Tikka is an Indian dish. The masala sauce was added to satisfy the desire of British people to have their meat served in gravy. Coming to terms with multiculturalism as a positive force for our economy and society will have significant implications for our understanding of Britishness.[15]

Food critics immediately pointed to the fact that choosing this dish was not an example of British's multiculturalism but their ignorance and an example of their habit of reducing foreign foods to unappetizing and inedible forms. As if chicken tikka wasn't diluted enough, the 'masala' part came in when diners complained that the tikka was rather too dry and that it had to be smeared in a sauce made of Campbell tomato soup, cream and spices.[16]

Sadly, even with the internet being a prime source of information sharing, there being ease of travel and availability of recipe archives and brilliant Indian cookbooks, London (and the world) is far from the knowledge of cuisines like Bhopali, Marwari, Bihari, Sikkimese, Kutchi—which form a huge part of Indian cuisine. In fact, even within these regions in India, eateries rarely dish out native food and one has to score a meal at a local's home to understand its nuances.

Back in India, in 1903, the Taj Mahal Hotel opened in Colaba, Mumbai, and changed the face of dining for the upper classes. It housed India's first licensed bar, The Harbour Bar, the first all-day restaurant Shamiana and the first discotheque,

Blow Up. Shamiana was one of the first restaurants to put local foods like pav bhaji on a restaurant menu as also the first to serve idlis and dosas on the breakfast menu versus eggs and waffles.[17] Think gulab jamun flambe and baked gajar ka halwa, alongside meat with brown sauce and imported grilled fish. This is in general five-star food. Recently, in 2020, when the hotel did a throwback to show their menu from the Independence Day banquet of 1947, one got to see what the night of freedom tasted like. This particular menu featured Indo-French cuisine, which was all the rage in the 1940s. For this dinner, its courses had as 'consomme a l'Indienne', a cardamom-infused clear soup; 'veloute d'amandes', a creamy almond soup; 'delices a l'Hindustan', meaning 'delicacies of India' and was interpreted as cottage cheese tikkas with mint chutney; 'paupiette de saumon joinville', salmon roulade served with wilted spinach, vegetables and joinville sauce; 'poularde souffle independence', chicken souffle with steamed vegetables and lemon sauce; and 'vacheris de peches Liberation', a dessert with peaches and meringue.

The 1900s saw the first official wave of modern Indian restaurants. This meant fine-tuned authentic dishes, presented to a diner in a sanitized setting. The Taj Mahal Hotel launched Tanjore in 1973, one of the first restaurants to serve pan-Indian food, while most other establishments were only offering Punjabi cuisine. In 1985, ITC Hotels launched in Chennai and two years later, in 1987, launched the first Bukhara in Delhi. Bukhara is known as one of the most iconic Indian restaurants the world over even today. While Bukhara dabbled

in North-West Indian cuisine, it remained as close as possible
to the food of the nation—certainly no diluted curries. Still
there was much more ground to be covered.

Some real experimentation was happening in Indian
restaurants in London. In 1982, the Taj International Hotels
in London, led by Camellia Punjabi, opened The Bombay
Brasserie. The restaurant had influences pouring in from
Goan, Bengali and Gujarati cuisine, along with Mughal,
British and Portuguese influences. 'Prior to Bombay Brasserie,
Indian restaurants did not exist, only curry houses. The only
middle-end restaurant was Gaylord in Mayfair. There were
also a couple of good Pakistani restaurants in Knightsbridge,'
she said in an interview.[18] Punjabi was in charge of marketing
and conceptualizing restaurants at the Taj, and it was she
who put sev puri on the London restaurant's menu, while in
India, she got them to explore Goan, Mangalorean and Kerala
cuisine and pushed them to move past cliched gravies from
north India and idli and dosa from the south.[19]

Today, she runs three successful Indian restaurants in
London: Amaya, Chutney Mary and Veeraswamy's, and
several Masala Zones with her sister Namita and her husband
Ranjit Mathrani. Her movement was topped by a number of
other Indian restaurants that opened in the city like Dishoom,
Gymkhana, Bombay Bustle, Hopper, Darjeeling Express,
Kricket, Trishna, Kama by Vineet and Quilon, the first south
Indian restaurant in the world to win a Michelin star.

While London's Indian food scene—notoriously compared
to Mumbai and Delhi's—continued to soar, Bangkok, New

York, Singapore and Dubai began talking the talk too. Since 2012, chef Vikas Khanna's restaurant Junoon in New York has won a Michelin star for six consecutive years. In 2018, chef Garima Arora became the first Indian woman to get a Michelin star for her Bangkok-based restaurant, Gaa. In 2019, Gaggan Bangkok, run by Indian chef Gaggan Anand in Thailand, was named the fourth-best restaurant in the world, and for four years in a row (2014–2018), it was voted as number one in Asia's 50 Best Restaurants. There is also a steady rise of Indian faces and food stores in the USA, with restaurants (Sona, Adda, Chai Pani, Botiwalla, Badmaash, Ghee Indian Kitchen, August 1 Five) and young food retailers (Brooklyn Delhi, Malai, Diaspora Co, Sach Foods) all championing Indian cuisine and produce.

Which brings me to Indian food in India. Redefining the cuisine right now are modern Indian restaurants like the Indian Accent, Masque, Bombay Canteen, O Pedro, Ziya and Avartana to name just a handful. Each restaurant here is redefining the generic understanding of Indian cuisine and there are a few points that tie them together. These restaurants refuse to cow down to preset rules of Indian cooking. While there is ample respect for roots and recipes, no experiment is high-risk enough. They work with more than one cuisine (for example, Mexican-Indian, Portuguese-Goan), have a deep co-dependent relationship with their farmers and producers, with absolute transparency about where ingredients come from and how the waste is utilized, borrow cooking techniques from other cuisines and their plating and seating focuses on comfort versus intimidation.

This is not the first time in Indian history that diners are at the brink of a colossal shift in their attitude towards cuisine. But this is definitely that time for my generation when we are witnessing a revision in approach. While concepts like chaat or kebab rolls would be considered lowbrow and fit for the streets, fine-dining restaurants have unequivocally embraced every facet of Indian cuisine. So, for me, new Indian food is dropping old stories and stereotypes, it is invested in finding a new rendition of itself, it is looking to rebel with a cause, guard its history and is in a constant mood for exploration. Indian cuisine is beginning to have a definitive voice.

ACKNOWLEDGEMENT

I feel so much gratitude for my family, mom, dad, Leena and Parag Mehta. For Ananya, whose love for books makes me want to write more books.

For my mentors Dr Shantilal Dedhia and Deenal Sampat.

For my friend Reva Goyal, who multitasked as my fact-checker and the first reader of all my drafts.

My editor Tarini Uppal, for being my biggest critic and fangirl. For giving me an opportunity to write this book that I hope will educate and inspire the generations to come.

And finally, as Snoop Dogg says: 'I want to thank me for believing in me.'

REFERENCES

Introduction

1. Nair, S. (2016, December 8). 'Do you know how ancient terracotta pottery actually is?' The Ethnic Soul. https://www.craftsvilla.com/blog/terracotta-pottery-history-art/.
2. NDTV Food. (3 April 2018). 'Here's why eating food with hands is a healthy habit'. Retrieved from https://food.ndtv.com/health/heres-why-eating-food-with-hands-is-a-healthy-habit-1831872.
3. McDermott, A. (n.d.). 'Arkaim: Aryans, advanced astronomy and untold secrets of a Russian citadel'. Retrieved from https://www.ancient-origins.net/ancient-places-asia/arkaim-aryans-advanced-astronomy-and-untold-secrets-russian-citadel-0010055.
4. Staff, H. (21 November 2018). 'Dalit identity and food—memories of trauma on a plate'. Retrieved 24 February 2021, from

https://homegrown.co.in/article/803216/dalit-identity-and-food-memories-of-trauma-on-a-plate.

5. Sunday Guardian Live. (26 August 2016). 'Dalit foods, an e-commerce enterprise that links the culinary with the political'. Retrieved from https://www.sundayguardianlive.com/people-society/6104-dalit-foods-e-commerce-enterprise-links-culinary-political.

6. Rudrappa, P. (15 November 2020). 'Govardhan Puja 2020: Date, time and significance'. Retrieved from https://www.ndtv.com/india-news/govardhan-puja-2020-its-significance-and-timings-2325386.

7. Staff, D. (13 May 2019). 'Right eating: What the Buddha taught'. Retrieved from https://www.dharmavoicesforanimals.org/eating/.

8. Sen, C.T. (2016). *Feasts and fasts: A history of food in India*. New Delhi: Speaking Tiger.

9. Someśvara and Shrigondekar, G.K. (1967). *Manasollasa of King Bhulokamalla Somesvara*, vol 1. Baroda: Oriental Institute.

10. Sadhale, N., and Nene, Y.L. (n.d.). 'On fish in Manasollasa'. Retrieved from https://www.asianagrihistory.org/pdf/articles/fish_article.pdf.

11. Burde, Jyotsna. (1963). 'Food and food habits in Vijayanagara times'. Kamat Research Database. Retrieved from http://www.kamat.com/database/articles/vnagar_foods.htm.

12. Achaya, K.T. (2014). *Indian food: A historical companion*. New Delhi: Oxford University Press.

13. 'Boundless world history'. (n.d) Retrieved from https://courses.lumenlearning.com/boundless-worldhistory/chapter/the-maurya-empire.

14. Spengler, R.N. (2019). *Fruit from the sands: The Silk Road origins of the foods we eat*. Oakland, CA: University of California Press.

15. Hendrix, S. (9 October 2018). 'Christopher Columbus and the potato that changed the world'. Retrieved from https://www.

washingtonpost.com/history/2018/10/08/christopher-columbus-potato-that-changed-world/.

16. Reza, S. (21 January 2015). 'A short history of the samosa'. Retrieved from https://scroll.in/article/701243/a-short-history-of-the-samosa.

17. Dar, K.P., and Dar, S. (1996). *Kashmiri cooking*. Penguin Books.

18. Grew, R. (2019). *Food in global history*. S.L.: Routledge.

Chapter 1: The Indus Valley

1. Parpola, A. (2015). *The roots of Hinduism: The early Aryans and the Indus civilization*. New York: Oxford University Press.

2. 'Grape'. (n.d.). Retrieved from http://nhb.gov.in/horticulture crops/grape/grape1.htm.

3. 'A brief introduction to the ancient Indus civilization'. (n.d.). Retrieved from https://www.harappa.com/har/indus-saraswati.html.

4. Burke Museum. (n.d.). 'Dance of the giant continents'. Retrieved from https://www.burkemuseum.org/geo_history_wa/Dance of the Giant Continents.htm.

5. *Plate Tectonics*. The Geological Society. Continental/continental: The Himalayas (n.d.). https://www.geolsoc.org.uk/Plate-Tectonics/Chap3-Plate-Margins/Convergent/Continental-Collision.

6. Joseph, T. (2018). *Early Indians: The story of our ancestors and where we came from*. New Delhi: Juggernaut.

7. Reich, David. (n.d.). 'Steppe migration to India was between 3500–4000 years ago'. Retrieved from https://economictimes.indiatimes.com/news/science/steppe-migration-to-india-was-between-3500-4000-years-ago-david-reich/articleshow/71556277.cms?from=mdr.

8. Kumar, Sajjan. (2012). 'Domestic animals in Harappan levels: Archaeological evidences'. In 'Domestication of animals in

Harappan culture: A socio–economic study (unpublished PhD diss.)'. Retrieved from https://shodhganga.inflibnet.ac.in/bitstream/10603/7817/10/10_chapter 3.pdf.

9. Hirst, K. Kris. (2020). 'Mehrgarh, Pakistan and life in the Indus valley before Harappa'. Retrieved from ThoughtCo, thoughtco.com/mehrgarh-pakistan-life-indus-valley-171796.

10. Encyclopedia.com. (n.d.). 'Indus valley'. Retrieved from https://www.encyclopedia.com/food/encyclopedias-almanacs-transcripts-and-maps/indus-valley.

11. Britannica. (n.d.). 'The Indian subcontinent'. Retrieved from https://www.britannica.com/topic/agriculture/The-Indian-subcontinent.

12. Meadow, R.H. (1981). *Early animal domestication in south Asia: A first report of the faunal remains from Mehrgarh, Pakistan.* In South Asian Archaeology 1979, edited by H. Hartel. Dietrich Reimer: Verlag, Berlin, 143–79.

13. Britannica. (n.d.). 'The Indian subcontinent'. Retrieved from https://www.britannica.com/topic/agriculture/The-Indian-subcontinent.

14. Cultural India. (n.d.) 'Indus valley civilization'. Retrieved from https://www.culturalindia.net/indian-history/ancient-india/indus-valley.html.

15. Misra, V. (n.d.). 'Prehistoric human colonization of India'. Retrieved from https://www.ias.ac.in/article/fulltext/jbsc/026/04/0491-0531.

16. Bhaduri, Sudarshana. (2005). 'Granaries in the Harappan civilization'. In 'Granaries and related systems of storage of crops in ancient India upto cAD 550 (unpublished PhD diss.)'. Retrieved from https://shodhganga.inflibnet.ac.in/bitstream/10603/155991/7/07_chapter 3.pdf.

17. InTeGrate. (25 January 2018). 'Geographical sites and ecological components of agricultural domestication'. Retrieved from https://serc.carleton.edu/integrate/teaching_materials/food_supply/student_materials/1135.

18. Hirst, K. (n.d.). 'The Indus valley civilization's gift to the world: Sesame seeds'. Retrieved from https://www.thoughtco.com/domestication-of-sesame-seed-169377.

19. Maestri, N. (n.d.) 'The four different ancient strands of cotton domestication'. Retrieved from https://www.thoughtco.com/domestication-history-of-cotton-gossypium-170429.

20. Weber, S. (n.d.). 'Seeds of urbanism: Palaeoethnobotany and the Indus civilization'. Retrieved from http://www.homepages.ucl.ac.uk/~tcrndfu/articles/orignal Weber antiquity.pdf.

21. Banerjee, S. (2016). 'Cooking the world's oldest known curry'. Retrieved from https://www.bbc.com/news/world-asia-india-36415079.

22. Lawler, A. (2013). 'The mystery of curry'. Retrieved from https://slate.com/human-interest/2013/01/indus-civilization-food-how-scientists-are-figuring-out-what-curry-was-like-4500-years-ago.html.

23. Desk, N. (10 December 2020). 'Dominance of meat in the diet of people in Indus valley civilisation, says new study'. Retrieved from https://www.nationalheraldindia.com/india/dominance-of-meat-in-the-diet-of-people-indus-valley-civilisation-says-new-study.

24. Kumar, Sajjan. (2012). 'Domestic animals in Harappan levels: Archaeological evidences'. In 'Domestication of animals in Harappan culture: a socio–economic study (unpublished PhD diss.)'. Retrieved from https://shodhganga.inflibnet.ac.in/bitstream/10603/7817/10/10_chapter 3.pdf.

25. Weber, S. (n.d.). 'Seeds of urbanism: Palaeoethnobotany and the Indus civilization'. Retrieved from http://www.homepages.ucl.ac.uk/~tcrndfu/articles/orignal Weber antiquity.pdf.

Chapter 2: The Impact of Religion

1. Brereton, J.P., and Jamison, S.W. (2014). *The Rigveda: The earliest religious poetry of India.* New York: Oxford University Press.

2. Bapat, G. (1966). 'Madhu-drinking: An interesting episode and problem from the Ramayana'. *Bulletin of the Deccan College Research Institute, 25*: 59–64. Retrieved from http://www.jstor.org/stable/42930838.

3. Cultural India. (n.d.). 'Vedic age'. Retrieved from https://www.culturalindia.net/indian-history/ancient-india/vedic-civilization.html.

4. Sashi and Dunsford, V. (12 March 2020). 'The four Vedas—origin and brief description of 4 Vedas'. Retrieved from https://vedicfeed.com/the-four-vedas/.

5. Thapar, R. (2003). *The Penguin history of early India: From the origins to AD 1300*. London: Penguin.

6. Achaya, K.T. (2000). *The story of our food*. Hyderabad, A.P.: Universities Press (India).

7. K.N. Sreeja. (2016). 'Food history as reflected in Sanskrit literature'. In 'Dietetics and culinary art in ancient and medieval India: A study with special reference to bhojanakutuhala (unpublished PhD diss.)'. Retrieved from https://shodhganga.inflibnet.ac.in/bitstream/10603/145416/8/08_chapter2.pdf.

8. Sen, C.T. (7 June 2019). 'Tracing India's food journey—from the Vedas'. Retrieved from https://www.livehistoryindia.com/history-in-a-dish/2018/05/12/tracing-indias-food-journey-from-the-vedas.

9. Kodlady N. 2014. 'The "*Pāka darpaṇam*": The text on Indian cookery by King Nala'. *Ancient Science of Life*, 33(4): 259–62.

10. Scribd. (n.d.). *Indian food and Cuisine Rekha Pande*. Scribd. https://www.scribd.com/document/370396441/Indian-Food-and-Cuisine-Rekha-Pande.

11. Achaya, K.T. (2000). *The story of our food*. Hyderabad, A.P.: Universities Press (India).

12. K.N. Sreeja. (2016). 'Food history as reflected in Sanskrit literature'. In 'Dietetics and culinary art in ancient and medieval India: A study with special reference to bhojanakutuhala (unpublished

PhD diss.)'. Retrieved from https://shodhganga.inflibnet.ac.in/bitstream/10603/145416/8/08_chapter2.pdf.

13. Sen, C.T. (7 June 2019). 'Tracing India's food journey—from the Vedas'. Retrieved from https://www.livehistoryindia.com/history-in-a-dish/2018/05/12/tracing-indias-food-journey-from-the-vedas.

14. Achaya, K.T. (2000). *The story of our food.* Hyderabad, A.P.: Universities Press (India).

15. Achaya, K.T. (2000). *The story of our food.* Hyderabad, A.P.: Universities Press (India).

16. Sen, C. (7 June 2019). 'Tracing India's food journey—from the Vedas'. Retrieved 25 February 2021, from https://www.livehistoryindia.com/history-in-a-dish/2018/05/12/tracing-indias-food-journey-from-the-vedas.

17. Deependra Yadav and SP Singh (2018). 'Vegetative methods of plant propagation: I-cutting layering and budding'. *Journal of Pharmacognosy and Phytochemistry*, 7(2): 3267–73.

18. Deependra Yadav and SP Singh (2018). 'Vegetative methods of plant propagation: I-cutting layering and budding'. *Journal of Pharmacognosy and Phytochemistry*, 7(2): 3267–73.

19. Deependra Yadav and SP Singh (2018). 'Vegetative methods of plant propagation: I-cutting layering and budding'. *Journal of Pharmacognosy and Phytochemistry*, 7(2): 3267–73.

20. Achaya, K.T. (2000). *The story of our food.* Hyderabad, A.P.: Universities Press (India).

21. Gopal, L. (1964). 'Sugar-making in ancient India'. *Journal of the Economic and Social History of the Orient*, 7(1–3): 57–72. doi: 10.1163/156852064x00030.

22. Gopal, L. (1964). 'Sugar-making in ancient India'. *Journal of the Economic and Social History of the Orient*, 7(1–3): 57–72. doi: 10.1163/156852064x00030.

23. Kalyanaraman, S. (n.d.). 'Itihāsa pariplava darśana narratives in Aśvamedha, mission of sovereignty, wealth acquisition'. Retrieved

from https://www.academia.edu/31040274/Itihāsa_pariplava_
darśana_narratives_in_Aśvamedha_mission_of_sovereignty_
wealth_acquisition. (n.d.).

24. Prabhu, M. (28 June 2017). 'The secret of the Soma plant'.
Retrieved from https://www.vedanet.com/the-secret-of-the-soma-
plant/.

25. Prabhu, M. (28 June 2017). 'The secret of the Soma plant'.
Retrieved from https://www.vedanet.com/the-secret-of-the-soma-
plant/.

26. Prabhu, M. (28 June 2017). 'The secret of the Soma plant'.
Retrieved from https://www.vedanet.com/the-secret-of-the-soma-
plant/.

27. Prabhu, M. (28 June 2017). 'The secret of the Soma plant'.
Retrieved from https://www.vedanet.com/the-secret-of-the-soma-
plant/.

28. Sarkar, P., D.H. C., Dhumal, S., and Panigrahi, R. (28 August
2015). 'Traditional and Ayurvedic foods of Indian origin'.
Retrieved from https://www.sciencedirect.com/science/article/
pii/S2352618115000438#:~:text=Traditionally%2C%20
Indian%20foods%20are%20classified%20into%20three%20
main%20categories.&text=Food%20is%20specific%20to%20
season,and%20shishira%20ritu%20(winter).

29. Ghosh, M.M. (17 June 2018). 'Eat, drink and be moderate:
Charaka advised the good life, not an assortment of pills'.
Retrieved from https://scroll.in/article/882866/eat-drink-and-
be-moderate-charaka-advised-the-good-life-not-an-assortment-
of-pill.

30. Sharma, P.V. (n.d.). *Charaka Samhita: Sanskrit text with an english
translation* (Vols 1–6).

31. Ghosh, M.M. (17 June 2018). 'Eat, drink and be moderate:
Charaka advised the good life, not an assortment of pills'. Retrieved
from https://scroll.in/article/882866/eat-drink-and-be-moderate-
charaka-advised-the-good-life-not-an-assortment-of-pills.

32. Sarkar, P., D.H.C., Dhumal, S., and Panigrahi, R. (28 August 2015). 'Traditional and Ayurvedic foods of Indian origin'. Retrieved from https://www.sciencedirect.com/science/article/pii/S2352618115000438#:~:text=Traditionally%2C%20Indian%20foods%20are%20classified%20into%20three%20main%20categories.&text=Food%20is%20specific%20to%20season,and%20shishira%20ritu%20(winter).

33. Pattanaik, D. (2013). *Sita: An illustrated retelling of the Ramayana.* Gurugram: Penguin Books.

34. Kodlady N. 2014. 'The "Pāka darpaṇam"': The text on Indian cookery by King Nala'. *Ancient Science of Life*, 33(4): 259–62.

35. 'Rishabhdev (Aadinath) swami'. (n.d.). Retrieved from http://en.encyclopediaofjainism.com/index.php/01._Rishabhdev_(Aadinath)_Swami.

36. Interview with Professor Muni Mahendra Kumar, Professor Emeritus, Jain Vishva Bharati Institute, Ladnun, Rajasthan.

37. Interview with Professor Muni Mahendra Kumar, Professor Emeritus, Jain Vishva Bharati Institute, Ladnun, Rajasthan.

38. Interview with Professor Muni Mahendra Kumar, Professor Emeritus, Jain Vishva Bharati Institute, Ladnun, Rajasthan.

39. Interview with Professor Muni Mahendra Kumar, Professor Emeritus, Jain Vishva Bharati Institute, Ladnun, Rajasthan.

40. Bailey, G. (2006). *The sociology of early Buddhism.* Cambridge: Cambridge University Press.

41. Cāttanār, Alain, Daniélou and Iyer, T.V. Gopal. (1993). *Manimekhalaï: The dancer with the magic bowl.* New Delhi: Penguin Books.

42. Stevens, J. (1985). 'What kind of food did Sakyamuni Buddha eat? summary'. *Journal of Indian and Buddhist Studies (Indogaku Bukkyogaku Kenkyu)*, 34(1): 441–44. doi: https://www.jstage.jst.go.jp/article/ibk1952/34/1/34_1_444/_pdf/-char/ja.

43. Stevens, J. (1985). 'What kind of food did Sakyamuni Buddha eat? summary'. *Journal of Indian and Buddhist Studies (Indogaku*

Bukkyogaku Kenkyu), 34(1): 441–44. doi: https://www.jstage.jst.
go.jp/article/ibk1952/34/1/34_1_444/_pdf/-char/ja

44. Stevens, J. (1985). 'What kind of food did Sakyamuni Buddha
eat? summary'. *Journal of Indian and Buddhist Studies (Indogaku
Bukkyogaku Kenkyu)*, 34(1): 441–44. doi: https://www.jstage.jst.
go.jp/article/ibk1952/34/1/34_1_444/_pdf/-char/ja.

45. Davids, T. W. R. (2000). *Buddhist birth stories: The oldest collection
of folk-lore extant*. United Kingdom: Routledge.

Chapter 3: Indian Royalty

1. Anwar, S. (23 May 2016). 'Peshwas under Maratha empire:
Detailed overview'. Retrieved from https://www.jagranjosh.com/
general-knowledge/peshwas-under-maratha-empire-detailed-
overview-1442579373-1.

2. Drishti IAS. (22 October 2019). 'Mauryan art and architecture-
part 1'. Retrieved from https://www.drishtiias.com/to-the-points/
paper1/mauryan-art-and-architecture-part-1.

3. Gopal, L., and Srivastava, V.C. (2008). *History of agriculture
in India, up to c. 1200 A.D.* New Delhi: Project of History of
Indian Science, Philosophy and Culture, Centre for Studies in
Civilizations.

4. Kautilya, and Sastry, R.S. (2020). *Kautilyas Arthashastra*. New
Delhi: Global Vision Publishing House.

5. Chanakya, A. (n.d.). *Chanakya Neeti, Sutras and Kautilya
Arthashastra (with Chanakya's biography)*. Tulsi Sahitya
Publications.

6. Kautilya, and Sastry, R.S. (2020). *Kautilyas Arthashastra*. New
Delhi: Global Vision Publishing House.

7. Kautilya, and Sastry, R.S. (2020). *Kautilyas Arthashastra*. New
Delhi: Global Vision Publishing House.

8. Kautilya, and Sastry, R.S. (2020). *Kautilyas Arthashastra*. New
Delhi: Global Vision Publishing House.

9. Kautilya, and Sastry, R.S. (2020). *Kautilyas Arthashastra*. New Delhi: Global Vision Publishing House.
10. Kautilya, and Sastry, R.S. (2020). *Kautilyas Arthashastra*. New Delhi: Global Vision Publishing House.
11. Mark, J.J. (8 May 2020). 'Hellenic world'. Retrieved from https://www.ancient.eu/Hellenic_World/.
12. Encyclopaedia Britannica. (18 January 2018). 'Pallava dynasty'. Retrieved from https://www.britannica.com/topic/Pallava-dynasty.
13. Yesodharan, D. (6 September 2017). 'From tortoise meat to roasted peppery goat, the Cholas of south India revelled in feasting'. Retrieved from https://www.huffingtonpost.in/devi-yesodharan/from-tortoise-meat-to-roasted-peppery-goat-the-cholas-of-south_a_23198572/?guccounter=1&guce_referrer=aHR0cHM6Ly93d3cuZ29vZ2xlLmNvbvS88&guce_referrer_sig=AQAAAFt0o63yjybbYqATn2Rv-rIxKzLOE1sEWTHrgjP4JMX4NpZtpEbHHLYo_HGDl8tUhXEZOzbHswTbSEnwTVqt9iczEGtEzZ3qk_M_dCmE55EKlI0UCjJWiYcu00Bf_1e_FsdZuHVxbE_0_QpUaJrryhwvBWYONOhFea1WRuxzMJuo.
14. Yesodharan, D. (6 September 2017). 'From tortoise meat to roasted peppery goat, the Cholas of south India revelled in feasting'. Retrieved from https://www.huffingtonpost.in/devi-yesodharan/from-tortoise-meat-to-roasted-peppery-goat-the-cholas-of-south_a_23198572/?guccounter=1&guce_referrer=aHR0cHM6Ly93d3cuZ29vZ2xlLmNvbvS88&guce_referrer_sig=AQAAAFt0o63yjybbYqATn2Rv-rIxKzLOE1sEWTHrgjP4JMX4NpZtpEbHHLYo_HGDl8tUhXEZOzbHswTbSEnwTVqt9iczEGtEzZ3qk_M_dCmE55EKlI0UCjJWiYcu00Bf_1e_FsdZuHVxbE_0_QpUaJrryhwvBWYONOhFea1WRuxzMJuo.
15. Saravanan, T. (10 September 2015). 'Royal recipes'. Retrieved from https://www.thehindu.com/features/metroplus/Food/n-

selvaraju-clinician-madurai-veterinary-poly-clinic-photo-r-ashok/article7637130.ece.

16. Vacek, J., Pieruccini, C., and Rossi, P. M. (2018). *A world of nourishment: Reflections on food in Indian culture.* Charles University, Prague.

17. Eraly, A. (2014). *The First Spring* Part 1: *Life in the Golden Age of India.* India: Penguin Books Limited.

18. Chelliah, J. V. (1985). *Pattupattu: Ten Tamil idylls.* Thanjavur: Tamil University.

19. Chelliah, J.V. (1985). *Pattupattu: Ten Tamil idylls.* Thanjavur: Tamil University.

20. David, S. (1980). *The epic structure: A critical study of Cīvaka Cintāmani as an epic.* Trivandrum: St. Josephs Press.

21. Cāttaṉār, Alain, Daniélou and Iyer, T.V. Gopal. (1993). *Manimekhalaï: The dancer with the magic bowl.* New Delhi: Penguin Books.

22. 'Vijaynagar empire'. (5 April 2018). Retrieved February 26, 2021, from https://andhrapradesh.pscnotes.com/history-of-india/vijaynagar-empire/#:~:text=The%20Vijayanagara%20Empire%2C%20an%20important,of%20Talikota%20in%201565%20AD.

23. Ganeshaiah, K.N., Shaanker, R.U., and Vasudeva, R. (n.d.). *Bio-resources and empire building: What favoured the growth of Vijayanagara empire?* Retrieved from http://repository.ias.ac.in/55518/1/28_pub.pdf.

24. Alcock, S.E., Daltroy, T.N., Morrison, K.D., and Sinopoli, C.M. (2009). *Empires: Perspectives from archaeology and history.* Cambridge: Cambridge University Press.

25. Burde, Jyotsna. (1963). 'Food and food habits in Vijayanagara times'. Kamat Research Database, retrieved from http://www.kamat.com/database/articles/vnagar_foods.htm.

26. Burde, Jyotsna. (1963). 'Food and food habits in Vijayanagara times'. Kamat Research Database, retrieved from http://www.kamat.com/database/articles/vnagar_foods.htm.

27. Burde, Jyotsna. (1963). 'Food and food habits in Vijayanagara times'. Kamat Research Database, retrieved from http://www.kamat.com/database/articles/vnagar_foods.htm.

28. Burde, Jyotsna. (1963). 'Food and food habits in Vijayanagara times'. Kamat Research Database, retrieved from http://www.kamat.com/database/articles/vnagar_foods.htm.

29. Burde, Jyotsna. (n.d). 'Food and food habits in Vijayanagara times'. Retrieved 26 February 2021, from https://defenceforumindia.com/threads/food-and-food-habits-in-vijayanagara-times.53818/.

30. Achaya, K.T. (2014). *Indian Food: A historical companion.* New Delhi: Oxford University Press.

31. Achaya, K.T. (2014). *Indian food: A historical companion.* New Delhi: Oxford University Press.

32. Achaya, K.T. (2014). *Indian food: A historical companion.* New Delhi: Oxford University Press.

33. 'Express: RoundGlass collective'. (n.d.). Retrieved from https://collective.round.glass/thali/thanjavur-maratha-cuisine.

34. Natarajan, P. (n.d.). 'The story of sambhar'. Retrieved from https://historytelling.files.wordpress.com/2013/07/the-story-of-sambhar-by-padmini-natarajan-e28094-archive-today.pdf.

35. Natarajan, P. (n.d.). 'The story of sambhar'. Retrieved from https://historytelling.files.wordpress.com/2013/07/the-story-of-sambhar-by-padmini-natarajan-e28094-archive-today.pdf.

36. Bhosle, P.S.S.R. (2017). *Contributions of Thanjavur Maratha kings: With a brief history of Chatrapathi Shivaji Maharaj, Dharmaveer Sambhaji Maharajah, Swami Samartha Ramdas, Cholas, Nayakas and Indian classical art-Bharatanatyam.* Chennai: Notion Press.

37. Rao, P.J. (2019). *Classic cuisine and celebrations of the Thanjavur Maharashtrians.* Notion Press.

38. Mehendale Aditya, and Swamy, M. (2015). *Rare gems: A non-vegetarian gourmet collection from Maharashtra.* Noida, Uttar Pradesh, India: Om Books International.

39. Interview with Yuvraj Mahanaaryaman Rao Scindia of Gwalior.

40. TheIndianTrip. (n.d.). 'Rajasthan experience guide—India information and tips on travel, tourism and FAQs'. Retrieved from https://theindiantrip.com/us/rajasthan-city/info.

41. Gurbaxani, G. (2018). *Jodhpur: An insight to a gourmet destination.* Notion Press.

42. Interview with Princess Siddhi Kumari.

43. Retrieved from Narendra Bhawan, Bikaner.

44. *The Bāgh o bahār; or, the garden and the spring; being the adventures of King Āzād Bakht and the four darweshes, literally translated from the Urdū of Mīr Amman, of Dihlī.* (1852). London: Sampson Low, Marston & Company.

45. *The Bāgh o bahār; or, the garden and the spring; being the adventures of King Āzād Bakht and the four darweshes, literally translated from the Urdū of Mīr Amman, of Dihlī.* (1852). London: Sampson Low, Marston & Company.

46. *The Bāgh o bahār; or, the garden and the spring; being the adventures of King Āzād Bakht and the four darweshes, literally translated from the Urdū of Mīr Amman, of Dihlī.* (1852). London: Sampson Low, Marston & Company.

47. Narayanan, D. (1 January 1970). *Cultures of food and gastronomy in Mughal and post-Mughal India.* UB Heidelberg. http://www.ub.uni-heidelberg.de/archiv/19906.

48. Narayanan, D. (1 January 1970). *Cultures of food and gastronomy in Mughal and post-Mughal India.* UB Heidelberg. http://www.ub.uni-heidelberg.de/archiv/19906.

49. Narayanan, D. (1 January 1970). *Cultures of food and gastronomy in Mughal and post-Mughal India.* UB Heidelberg. http://www.ub.uni-heidelberg.de/archiv/19906.

50. Narayanan, D. (1 January 1970). *Cultures of food and gastronomy in Mughal and post-Mughal India.* UB Heidelberg. http://www.ub.uni-heidelberg.de/archiv/19906.

51. Narayanan, D. (1 January 1970). *Cultures of food and gastronomy in Mughal and post-Mughal India*. UB Heidelberg. http://www.ub.uni-heidelberg.de/archiv/19906.

52. Mukherjee, S. (2001). *Royal Mughal ladies and their contributions*. New Delhi: Gyan Publishing House.

53. Narayanan, D. (n.d.). *Cultures of food and gastronomy in Mughal and post-Mughal India.*

54. *Hindustan Times.* (2 February 2019). 'Biryani: Ek khoj'. https://www.hindustantimes.com/brunch/biryani-ek-khoj/story-HZcKcXdFAZMWq9jltZrbhL.html.

55. Sen, S. (2019). *Ganga: The many pasts of a river.* Gurugram: Penguin Viking, an imprint of Penguin Random House.

56. Baseer, A.A. (9 February 2019). 'Aafiya Ayman Baseer'. Retrieved from http://www.hydnews.net/the-tales-and-theories-about-the-origin-of-chaat-snack/.

57. Baseer, A.A. (9 February 2019). 'Aafiya Ayman Baseer'. Retrieved from http://www.hydnews.net/the-tales-and-theories-about-the-origin-of-chaat-snack/.

58. Baseer, A.A. (9 February 2019). 'Aafiya Ayman Baseer'. Retrieved from http://www.hydnews.net/the-tales-and-theories-about-the-origin-of-chaat-snack/.

59. Pressreader.com. (n.d.). Retrieved 2 March 2021, from https://www.pressreader.com/india/business-standard/20171104/281741269687467.

60. Narayanan, D. (1 January 1970). *Cultures of food and gastronomy in Mughal and post-Mughal India.* UB Heidelberg. http://www.ub.uni-heidelberg.de/archiv/19906.

61. Narayanan, D. (1 January 1970). *Cultures of food and gastronomy in Mughal and post-Mughal India.* UB Heidelberg. http://www.ub.uni-heidelberg.de/archiv/19906.

62. Sen, C.T. (2016). *Feasts and fasts: A history of food in India.* New Delhi: Speaking Tiger.

63. Shah, A. (31 July 2019). 'Nimatnama—the treasure trove of recipes'. Retrieved from https://www.livehistoryindia.com/history-in-a-dish/2017/12/02/nimatnama--the-treasure-trove-of-recipes.

64. Pathak, Harsh. (14 April 2020). 'From Egypt to Libya and from central Asia to India, the humble samosa has come a long way—Gaonconnection: Your connection with rural India'. Retrieved from https://en.gaonconnection.com/from-egypt-to-libya-and-from-central-asia-to-india-the-humble-samosa-has-come-a-long-way-do-you-know-it-first-came-into-existence-in-the-10th-century/.

65. Gulbadan, Thackston, W.M., Jawhar, and Biyāt Bāyazīd. (2009). *Three memoirs of Humayun*. Costa Mesa, CA: Mazda Publishers.

66. Interview with Salma Yusuf Husain.

67. Yagnik, A., and Sheth, S. (2011). *Ahmedabad: From royal city to megacity*. New Delhi: Penguin Books.

68. Sharar, A.H., Hussain, F., and Harcourt, E.S. (2012). *Lucknow: The last phase of an oriental culture*. New Delhi: Oxford University Press.

69. Mishra, K.P. (1975). *Banaras in transition, (1738–1795): A socio-economic study*. New Delhi: Munshiram Manoharlal.

70. Interview with Salma Yusuf Husain.

71. Interview with Niloufer Rashiduzzafar Khan from the royal family of Bhopal.

72. Interview with Niloufer Rashiduzzafar Khan from the royal family of Bhopal.

73. Sen, C.T. (2016). *Feasts and fasts: A history of food in India*. New Delhi: Speaking Tiger.

Chapter 4: Traders and Conquerors

1. Reshii, M.H. (2017). *The flavour of spice: Journeys, recipes, stories*. Gurugram: Hachette India.

2. Stoneman, R. (2019). *The Greek experience of India: From Alexander to the Indo-Greeks*. Princeton, NJ: Princeton University Press.

3. Herodotus. 1862. *The History*, translated by George Rawlinson. New York: Dutton & Co. Scanned by J.S. Arkenberg, Department of History, California State Fullerton. Professor Arkenberg has modernized the text.

4. Herodotus. 1862. *The History*, translated by George Rawlinson. New York: Dutton & Co. Scanned by J.S. Arkenberg, Department of History, California State Fullerton. Professor Arkenberg has modernized the text.

5. Davids, T.W. (1890). *The questions of King Milinda*. Oxford: Clarendon Press.

6. Stoneman, R. (2019). *The Greek experience of India: From Alexander to the Indo-Greeks*. Princeton, NJ: Princeton University Press.

7. Stoneman, R. (2019). *The Greek experience of India: From Alexander to the Indo-Greeks*. Princeton, NJ: Princeton University Press.

8. Stoneman, R. (2019). *The Greek experience of India: From Alexander to the Indo-Greeks*. Princeton, NJ: Princeton University Press.

9. Frankopan, P. (2020). *The new silk roads: The new Asia and the remaking of the world order*. New York: Vintage Books, a division of Penguin Random House LLC.

10. Frankopan, P. (2020). *The new silk roads: The new Asia and the remaking of the world order*. New York: Vintage Books, a division of Penguin Random House LLC.

11. Apicius, and Vehling, J. D. (2009). *Cookery and dining in imperial Rome. Gutenberg*. Lightning Source. www.gutenberg.org.

12. Pliny. (2012). *Natural history*. London: Folio Society.

13. Elliott, L. (2004). *Food and feasts in the Middle Ages*. Crabtree Publishing Company.

14. Sri Lanka Export Development Board. (2 July 2015). 'The history of pure Ceylon cinnamon, the spice of life'. Retrieved from https://www.srilankabusiness.com/blog/history-of-spice-of-life.html.

15. Bernstein, W.J. (2009). *A splendid exchange: How trade shaped the world*. London: Distributed by Group West.

16. Lamont, W.J. (1999). *Okra—a versatile vegetable crop.* *HortTechnology*, 9(2): 179–184. doi:10.21273/horttech.9.2.179.
17. MacVeigh, J. (2008). *International Cuisine.* United States: Cengage Learning.
18. Coffee Board of India. (2004). *Indian coffee: Bulletin of the Indian coffee board,* vol. 68.
19. Polo, M., Komroff, M., and Marsden, W. (2013). *The travels of Marco Polo: The Venetian.* Breinigsville, PA: Nabu Press.
20. Elisseeff, V. (2000). *The silk roads: Highways of culture and commerce.* New York: Berghahan.
21. Athenaeus, and Yonge, C.D. (1854). *The Deipnosophists or banquet of the learned of Athenaeus: With an appendix of poetical fragments, rendered into English verse by various authors and a general index: In three volumes.* London: Bohn.
22. UNESCO. (April 2015). 'Sites along the Uttarapath, Badshahi Sadak, Sadak-e-Azam, Grand Trunk Road'. Retrieved from http://whc.unesco.org/en/tentativelists/6056.
23. Elisseeff, V. (2000). *The silk roads: Highways of culture and commerce.* New York: Berghahan.
24. Pant, Pushpesh. (2005). *Food path: Cuisine along the Grand Trunk Road from Kabul to Kolkata.* Roli Books Pvt Ltd, India.
25. Husihui, Buell, P.D., Anderson, E.N., and Perry, C. (2016). *A soup for the Qan: Chinese dietary medicine of the Mongol era as seen in Hu Szu-Hui's Yin-Shan Cheng-Yao: Introduction, translation, commentary, and Chinese text.* Oxon: Routledge.
26. 'The Yinshan Zhengyao'. (n.d.). Retrieved from https://ebrary.net/7722/geography/yinshan_hengyao.
27. Buell, P.D., Anderson, E.N., De, P.M., and Oskenbay, M. (2020). *Crossroads of cuisine the Eurasian heartland, the silk roads and food.* Leiden: Brill.
28. Spengler, R.N. (2019). *Fruit from the sands: The Silk Road origins of the foods we eat.* Oakland, CA: University of California Press.

29. Pearson, M.N. (1987). *The Portuguese in India*. Cambridge: Cambridge University Press.
30. Pearson, M.N. (1987). *The Portuguese in India*. Cambridge: Cambridge University Press.
31. MacVeigh, J. (2008). *International Cuisine*. United States: Cengage Learning.
32. Kiple, K.F., and Ornelas, K.C. (2000). *The Cambridge world history of food*. New York: Cambridge University Press.
33. 'Portuguese in Bengal: A history beyond slave trade'. (n.d.). Retrieved from https://www.sahapedia.org/portuguese-bengal-history-beyond-slave-trade.
34. Aneja, R. (2002). *Technology of Indian milk products: Handbook on process technology modernization for professionals, entrepreneurs, and scientists*. Delhi: Dairy India Yearbook.
35. Aneja, R. (2002). *Technology of Indian milk products: Handbook on process technology modernization for professionals, entrepreneurs, and scientists*. Delhi: Dairy India Yearbook.
36. 'Paneer—an Indian soft cheese variant: A review'. (n.d.). Retrieved from https://www.researchgate.net/publication/257798133_Paneer_-_An_Indian_soft_cheese_variant_A_review.
37. Hussain, R.K. (n.d.). 'Armenian, Iranian and Turkish merchants in India 1550–1800'. Retrieved from https://core.ac.uk/download/pdf/144511061.pdf.
38. 'Armenians in Bengal and cabbage dolma'. (n.d.). Retrieved from https://forktales.in/2019/08/18/armenians-in-bengal-and-cabbage-dolma/#:~:text=The%20Armenians%20are%20believed%20to,rice%20%E2%80%93%20with%20them%20to%20Bengal.&text=With%20the%20passage%20of%20time,in%20the%20elite%20Bengali%20kitchen.
39. O'Brien, C. (2013). *The Penguin food guide to India*. New Delhi: Penguin Books.
40. Marks, C. (1991). *The varied kitchens of India: Cuisines of the Anglo-Indians of Calcutta, Bengalis, Jews of Calcutta, Kashmiris,*

Parsis and Tibetans of Darjeeling. Lanham, Maryland: M Evans and Co Inc.

41. O'Brien, C. (2013). *The Penguin food guide to India.* New Delhi: Penguin Books.

42. Prakash, O. (2014). *The Dutch East India company and the economy of Bengal, 1630–1720.* Princeton University Press.

43. Koene, A.H. (2011). *Food shopper's guide to Holland: A comprehensive review of the finest local and international food products in the Dutch marketplace.* Delft: Eburon.

44. 'National coffee association'. (n.d.). Retrieved from https://www.ncausa.org/about-coffee/history-of-coffee.

45. Ovington, J, Rawlinson, H.G. (1994). *A voyage to Surat in the year 1689.* New Delhi: Asian Educational Services.

46. Baruah, P. (n.d.). 'Wild teas of Assam and north east India'. Retrieved from http://www.aquapublisher.com/index.php/jtsr/article/html/3179/.

47. Collingham, E.M. (2018). *The hungry empire: How Britain's quest for food shaped the modern world.* London: Vintage.

48. Saberi, H. (2013). *Tea: A global history.* London: Reaktion.

49. Chati, A. (12 July 2017). 'Punch: History in a bowl'. Retrieved from https://www.livehistoryindia.com/history-in-a-dish/2017/07/13/punch-history-in-a-bowl.

50. Brown, P. (2008). *Anglo-Indian food and customs: Tenth anniversary edition.* Bloomington, IN: IUniverse.

51. Brown, P. (2008). *Anglo-Indian food and customs: Tenth anniversary edition.* Bloomington, IN: IUniverse.

Chapter 5: Conclusion

1. Sharma, K. (2018, May 7). 'Rabindranath Tagore's love for food was almost as deep as his love for words'. Indian Women Blog—Stories of Indian Women. Retrieved from https://www.

indianwomenblog.org/rabindranath-tagores-love-for-food-was-almost-as-deep-as-his-love-for-words/.

2. Sharma, K. (2018, May 7). 'Rabindranath Tagore's love for food was almost as deep as his love for words'. Indian Women Blog—Stories of Indian Women. Retrieved from https://www.indianwomenblog.org/rabindranath-tagores-love-for-food-was-almost-as-deep-as-his-love-for-words/.

3. Sen, P. (2016, May 7). 'What would you serve Rabindranath Tagore if he came home for lunch?' *The Indian Express*. Retrieved from https://indianexpress.com/article/lifestyle/food-wine/what-would-you-serve-rabindranath-tagore-if-he-came-home-for-lunch-2788629/; Bengal Cuisine (N.d.). 'Tagorean Cuisine: Food Habits of Thakurbari'. Retrieved from https://www.bengalcuisine.in/tagorean_cuisine.

4. Gross, D. M. (2014). *99 tactics of successful tax resistance campaigns*. Picket Line Press.

5. Slate, N. (2019, February 22). 'Gandhi's vision for equality involved raw food'. The Atlantic. Retrieved from https://www.theatlantic.com/entertainment/archive/2019/02/gandhis-raw-food-diet/582721/.

6. Pritchett, F. (n.d.). 'Experiments in Dietetics'. Retrieved from http://www.columbia.edu/itc/mealac/pritchett/00litlinks/gandhi/part1/117chapter.html.

7. Ghoshal, S. (2019, August 9). 'Mahatma Gandhi's experiments with food'. Retrieved from mint. https://www.livemint.com/mint-lounge/features/mahatma-gandhi-s-experiments-with-food-1565337570842.html.

8. Vishal, A. (2016). *Mrs Lc's table: Stories about Kayasth food and culture*. Hachette India.

9. Deo, S.B. (2018, February 17). 'The impact of Partition on Delhi's food culture'. Shabd Braham. Retrieved from http://shabdbraham.com/ShabdB/archive/v6i3/sbd-v6-i3-sn30.pdf.

10. Vishal, A. (2017, August 14). 'Partition changed India's food cultures forever'. The Wire. Retrieved from https://thewire.in/food/partition-food-punjab-mughlai-bengal.

11. John, D.A., and Babu, G.R. (2021, February 22). 'Lessons from the aftermaths of Green Revolution on food system and health'. Frontiers in sustainable food systems. Retrieved from https://www.ncbi.nlm.nih.gov/pmc/articles/PMC7611098/.

12. Vadilal Group. (n.d.). 'History'. Retrieved from https://vadilalgroup.com/?page_id=124.

13. Bhushan, R. (2011, March 3). 'Parle-G world's No. 1 selling biscuit: Nielsen'. The Economic Times. Retrieved from https://economictimes.indiatimes.com/industry/cons-products/food/parle-g-worlds-no-1-selling-biscuit-nielsen/articleshow/7616188.cms?intenttarget=no.

14. Historic UK. (n.d.). 'History of the British curry'. Retrieved from https://www.historic-uk.com/CultureUK/The-British-Curry/.

15. Cook, R. (2001, April 19). 'Robin Cook's chicken tikka masala speech'. The Guardian. Retrieved from https://www.theguardian.com/world/2001/apr/19/race.britishidentity.

16. Collingham, E.M. (2006). Curry: A tale of cooks and conquerors. Oxford University Press.

17. Vir Sanghvi. (n.d.). 'Camellia Panjabi is the Queen of Indian food'. Retrieved from https://virsanghvi.com/Article-Details.aspx?key=909.

18. Lutrario, J. (2020, November 18). 'Chutney Mary at 30: How one restaurant changed London's Indian dining scene'. Retrieved from bighospitality.co.uk. https://www.bighospitality.co.uk/Article/2020/11/18/Chutney-Mary-Indian-restaurant-MW-Eat-Camellia-Panjabi.

19. Vir Sanghvi. (n.d.). 'Camellia Panjabi is the Queen of Indian food'. Retrieved from https://virsanghvi.com/Article-Details.aspx?key=909.